Praise for *The Elephant And The Mouse*

"Addressing diversity and inclusion is a global, societal, and moral issue of utmost importance. At Mercer, we take an evidence-based approach to solving diversity, equity, and inclusion challenges. As a people business, having colleagues with diverse backgrounds, perspectives, experiences, and cultures brings a richness of ideas that, in turn, helps us make brighter futures for everyone. Leaders need to be the north stars for their people, and they need to enable other leaders to support employees and execute DEI strategy through everyday actions. Companies are a large part of society with both the ability and the obligation to create progress across diversity, equity, and inclusion.

Laura Liswood's expertise in the fields and diversity of leadership is exceptional. We are fortunate to have her voice and her knowledge, as so eloquently shared in *The Elephant and the Mouse*. *The Elephant and the Mouse* outlines how we can understand both our conscious and unconscious biases and the ways they affect our perspectives and our decisions–both personally and professionally–across all facets of our lives. *The Elephant and the Mouse* shows the ways in which diversity alone is not enough and how we can all work together to help close the gaps between us.

Achieving true diversity, equity, and inclusion is an ongoing journey and educating ourselves is an important step. The insights in this book were revelatory to me as a friend, as a colleague, and as a leader but most importantly, as a human being. No matter who you are or where you are starting from, *The Elephant and the Mouse* contains lessons for everyone. It asks you to question yourself and provides a framework you can apply to your own life to actively shape change and transform the communities you are a part of. *The Elephant and the Mouse* illuminates the path forward to real and lasting change and I recommend it for everyone."

—**Martine Ferland,** President and CEO, Mercer

"If Laura Liswood ran the world, it would be a fairer, more inclusive place. In this wise book, she highlights that many of our problems with diversity stem not from differences in demography but from differences in power. Her analysis of dominant and non-dominant groups offers valuable tools to have more productive conversations and drive more meaningful progress."

—**Adam Grant,** #1 *New York Times* bestselling author of *Think Again* and host of the TED podcast *WorkLife*

"*The Elephant and Mouse* is a must-read for anyone committed to making their workplace or their community truly inclusive. *The Loudest Duck* synthesized all the diversity research and gave us a framework for how to understand our challenges to diversity and inclusion and was a game changer in our thinking. *The Elephant and Mouse* takes that to the next level in such an amazing way . . . to elevate our thinking in the way that only Laura can! Laura gives us a powerfully new framework to break through traditional approaches to social inclusion so that we can take our diversity efforts to the next level. Laura has that one-of-a-kind mind that shows us where we are—why we might be stuck—and gives us a practical framework to turn our good intentions into meaningful change and real impact."

—**Beth Brooke,** former Vice-Chair, EY

"Laura has done it again!

As the former Deputy Director for Diversity and Inclusion during the Obama Administration, we used Laura to train the entirety of Senior Executive Service leaders throughout the federal workspace based on her groundbreaking and hugely successful book, *The Loudest Duck: Moving Beyond Diversity While Embracing Differences to Achieve Success at Work.*

In *The Loudest Duck,* Laura gave senior leaders within the federal government practical tips and tools to harness cognitive diversity. Her senior leader sessions were nothing short of fantastic and received much acclaim. I loved *The Loudest Duck* so much I constantly use phrases I picked up from Laura like "Noah's Ark diversity" while speaking to various audiences. I never imagined that Laura could author a follow-on book that could rival the simple truths and penetrating insight of *The Loudest Duck,* but she has!

The Elephant and the Mouse is so good that I'm mad I didn't think of it.

In *The Elephant and the Mouse,* Laura provides a deep and transformative analysis of an issue at the heart of DEI. And that is the differing perceptions of dominant and non-dominant groups of organizational and societal lived experiences. Laura makes the brilliant point that dominant group members must work to understand, appreciate, and acknowledge the lived experiences of non-dominant group members such as women and people of color. In Laura's new book, you will learn hard truths about diversity and inclusion, why meritocracy as is currently understood is a myth, understand the real difference between the Model T and the Tesla, why we need to move beyond simple unconscious bias training, and so much more.

This book is simply one of the most important books on DEI I have read in recent years."

—**Bruce J. Stewart,** CEO, The Small World Group

"*The Elephant and the Mouse* tells us how ignorant we can be of each other, how group thinking can limit our horizon, and how we can so much improve by exploring, understanding, and sharing with the other tribe, if only because as La Fontaine reminds us in *The Lion and the Rat*: We need each other. There is a long way to go, and this book is a great start on the journey."

—**Christine Lagarde,** President, European Central Bank

the
Elephant
and the
Mouse

Moving Beyond the Illusion of Inclusion ᴛᴏ Create a Truly Diverse and Equitable Workplace

Laura Liswood
Author of *The Loudest Duck*

WILEY

Published by John Wiley & Sons, Inc., Hoboken, New Jersey.
Published simultaneously in Canada.

For general information on our other products and services or for technical support, please contact our Customer Care Department within the United States at (800) 762-2974, outside the United States at (317) 572-3993 or fax (317) 572-4002.

Wiley also publishes its books in a variety of electronic formats. Some content that appears in print may not be available in electronic formats. For more information about Wiley products, visit our web site at www.wiley.com.

Library of Congress Cataloging-in-Publication Data

Names: Liswood, Laura A., 1950- author. | John Wiley & Sons, publisher.
Title: The elephant and the mouse : Moving Beyond the Illusion of Inclusion to Create a Truly Diverse and Equitable Workplace / Laura Liswood.
Description: Hoboken, New Jersey : Wiley, [2022] | Includes index.
Identifiers: LCCN 2021052112 (print) | LCCN 2021052113 (ebook) | ISBN 9781119836254 (hardback) | ISBN 9781119836278 (adobe pdf) | ISBN 9781119836261 (epub)
Subjects: LCSH: Diversity in the workplace. | Organizational change—Management.
Classification: LCC HF5549.5.M5 L568 2022 (print) | LCC HF5549.5.M5 (ebook) | DDC 658.3008—dc23/eng/20211208
LC record available at https://lccn.loc.gov/2021052112
LC ebook record available at https://lccn.loc.gov/2021052113

COVER DESIGN: PAUL MCCARTHY
COVER ART: (ELEPHANT) © GETTY IMAGES | ABSODELS
(MOUSE) © SHUTTERSTOCK | CHOST BEAR

SKY10032947_020122

To my sister Jan, who will always be my north star.

Contents

Acknowledgments

My friend, dynamic businesswoman, and wonderful supporter Adrienne Arsht will say to me as we end a phone call or after a delightful dinner, "To be continued." This is how I feel about the journey that I have been on for diversity, equity, inclusion, and women's empowerment. The arc of my career always returns to these personal and professional passions.

It has been 10 years since I wrote *The Loudest Duck*, and to rephrase a French saying, the more things change, the more they stay the same. I celebrate the great progress that has been made in our diverse world. The fact that there is more call for wanting real change is heartening. When I was in college, I could not even think to be considered for a Rhodes scholarship or be admitted into a military academy. I probably would not have attained either of those goals, but the choice was not mine to seek. Today, young, talented, ambitious women can do so, and they know the contributions they can make.

However, the fact that less change has been made than many of us hoped falls into the "to be continued" category. In the book, I quote from the World Economic Forum *Global Gender Gap Report*. The gap continues and the date of its demise stretches further and further away. I want to acknowledge Saadia Zahidi, a managing director of the Forum, for her tireless work on gender and for making a global meeting place like Davos much more reflective of the achievements of women and others not automatically included. She ensures that women have a seat at the table and she continues to expand our knowledge of what equality looks like for all.

I like to write, but my writing often sounds the way I speak, with run-on sentences and looping bits of logic, full of less than succinct opinion. I must thank my editor Bridget Samburg, who worked with me on *The Loudest Duck* and now *The Elephant and the Mouse*. If these books are readable and of value, Bridget is one of the main reasons they are so.

I reread the acknowledgment pages of *The Loudest Duck* and I am grateful and relieved that many of the people I acknowledged then are the ones I feel the same way about now. The joy is that there are people who have entered my life and helped support my efforts on this journey and who have brought new thinking and impact to the diversity, equity, and inclusion world.

Scholars and practitioners whom I admire in this field, whom I have learned greatly from and quote here, have been continual supporters of mine. They include Herminia Ibarra, professor at the London Business School; Iris Bohnet from the Harvard Kennedy School of Government; Mark Kaplan and Mason Donovan of the

Dagoba Group; Kathleen McQuiggan from Artemis Financial Advisors; Kendall Wright, CEO of Entelechy; Steven Frost of Included; Beth Brooke, former vice chair of EY; Marques Benton, chief diversity officer of Loomis Sayles; Adam Grant, professor at Wharton School of Business, University of Pennsylvania; Joerg Schmitz at Thomas Leland. Rafael Polanco's and Brogiin Keeton's observations as practitioners help keep me grounded. This list is by no means exhaustive as I continually learn from those who embrace a passion for diversity, equity, and inclusion.

I especially admire the thousands of people who speak out, protest, and rightly demand a fair and respectful world.

In 2014 I retired from the Washington, D.C., Metropolitan Police Department as a reserve sergeant. I was proud to serve with my fellow officers, who strive to act to the highest standards that everyone deserves. I am disheartened by policing actions experienced by some communities and appreciative of those who see the need for systemic reform and who give voice to that need.

The cliché that no man (woman) is an island is true, at least in my lived experience. I have had unconditional support from many. It is unconditional in that my friends and family want to be present for me and also keep me from going too far down any rabbit holes I am inclined to fall into. This extended family that I was both born into and choose include my "sister" cousin Judy Liswood

Stokes and her husband, a noted leader in health care, Chuck Stokes. They and Josh, Joel, Neil and Sherry, David, Lidia, Ellen, Ken, Debby, and Dori are dear family to me. Adrienne, one of the most powerful and impactful women leaders I know has supported me in so many ways. Melody and Candace have been part of my chosen family for decades, along with Linda, Caitlin, Lew, Luke and Robert, Jim and Kathy, Natalie and Jim, Amy, Lily, Nik and Melissa, Mel S., the Hill family, and so many more family and friends.

Professionally, I am surrounded by an extraordinary team who always goes above and beyond in their efforts. The Council of Women World Leaders is a vibrant organization because of a dedicated group, including Patricia Deyton, Sarah Wildi, Caroline Wachtell, Claudia Boscan Medina, and Rachel Berman. Sarah gave a keen eye to the writing and Rachel was my research associate for this book.

John Wiley & Sons provided me a platform and a welcome that any author would want. Thank you to Deborah Schindler, Sally Baker, Shannon Vargo, John Skinner, and the design team, who were enthusiastic and embraced the value of diversity, inclusion, and equity.

Adobe continues to sit on my keyboard and Mao prefers his own company.

All errors, omissions, and mistakes are mine alone.

Introduction

Ten years ago, I wrote *The Loudest Duck: Moving Beyond Diversity While Embracing Differences to Achieve Success at Work* (Wiley & Sons). My work with organizations prompted me to write that initial book on diversity because I observed those same organizations struggling with how to both make a case for diversity and implement efforts to achieve what they said their goals were.

Ten years on, I do observe progress, particularly in the recognition that it isn't just about diversity, but must also encompass equity and inclusion. I called the initial focus on diversity the "Noah's Ark" phase. That's when you just get two of each in the ark and say you have accomplished the mission. Many groups are still in that stage, with representation of differing people the be-all and end-all of the efforts, mainly concentrating on recruitment of diverse individuals.

While recruiting was and is important, it is a partial view. It is the "intake" view, but it does not recognize the "upgrade" view or the inclusion and equity view. That is, people are coming in the door but have not been as successful at thriving and rising in organizations. It also did not take into account what is now clearly seen: that a new type of leadership is required, one that prizes inclusivity as an essential element of what leaders must do.

In *The Loudest Duck*, my purpose was to create clear and practical ways to ensure that people were treated equitably and that the value of diversity would be attained. The book started with a look at the case for diversity, particularly cognitive diversity and getting the differing perspectives that each of us brings to the workplace to enhance creativity and innovation. There are many other reasons for why diversity should be pursued, but at many points in the book I refer back to this fundamental reason. I ask the reader if they are getting the cognitive diversity they purport to want.

The next step was to explore what we unconsciously bring to the workplace, beyond unconscious bias that makes us respond to people who are like us differently than people who are not like us. I wanted to move beyond thinking only of unconscious bias to thinking of all the other types of unconscious ways of existing. We have unconscious beliefs, attitudes, perspectives, preferences, roles, associations, and archetypes.

I then focused on the Elephant and the Mouse, which is the concept that dominant groups know little about nondominant groups, but the latter knows a great deal about the former. This causes continual issues and problems within organizations because it means that some people have almost no awareness of how actions, processes, decisions, and comments can disproportionately impact diverse individuals.

Dominant groups still don't know the fully lived lives of nondominant groups. I have come to see that this dynamic is perhaps one of the most powerful ones that haunt societies, particularly as more and more diverse groups correctly express their desire to be fully accepted and treated equitably. The Elephant and Mouse metaphor has resonated well with those who read my book and those to whom I've spoken. In fact, it was so popular that one group decided to name its company The Mouse and the Elephant and base its framework on my work!

As the world continues to become increasingly interconnected, it is crucial to know about others, particularly how others experience life and are impacted by conscious and unconscious beliefs about who they are. That is why this book is titled *The Elephant and the Mouse*. To me, this is a core tenet of the effort to reach full diversity, equity, inclusion, and social justice. It now must be a core tenet of how leaders behave and how they are measured. Diversity, equity, and inclusion can no longer be seen as "nice to have" but are essential to high-functioning, successful organizations. A parallel example, given to me by Mason Donovan and Mark Kaplan of the Dagoba Group, might be when a company realizes that "safety first" requires a full reorientation of how it operates and how everyone is responsible for that safety goal.

The Elephant and the Mouse is a callout to all of us to acknowledge that the concepts and realities of diversity, inclusion, and equity are becoming fully embedded in our lives and structures. This requires far more from each of us with concomitant effort and reward.

THE DIVERSITY OF DIVERSITY

The Loudest Duck also outlined the many diversities we find in the workplace, not simply the legally covered or generally assumed ones such as gender, race, ethnicity, nationality, sexual orientation, disability, religion, or age. Diversity is about like to like and like to not like. We discover that there are many ways we separate ourselves from others. In that separation comes a propensity to bond and take seriously those who are like us and to distance ourselves or find reasons to dismiss others who are unlike us, as well as their ideas and even their essential personhood.

There are the smokers and the nonsmokers, introverts and extroverts, tall and short people, folks who are standard weight and those who are nonstandard weight. Introverts think that extroverts talk too much and extroverts think that introverts have nothing to say. There are the Manchester United football fans and the Arsenal fans, both equally passionate and, in their own minds, quite discerning. Parents and non-parents often live in different worlds from each other, and so too do those who have varying speaking styles.

Different nationalities can create troublesome beliefs and give permission to one group to dismiss the thinking and creativity of the other, thereby defeating what was the original stated rationale for diversity. In his book *Blink*, Malcolm Gladwell explains that 16% of men in the United States are 6 feet or taller, but 57% of Fortune 500 male CEOs are 6 feet or taller, which is four times the cohort![1] I have yet to see research that correlates leadership ability and skeletal structure.

The military has a convenient phrase: "Large and in charge." We have an image of what a leader looks like. If you fit that image, you have a lot of tailwinds going for you. People will assume you are competent until you prove you are not. If you are shorter than 6 feet tall, you are *not* going to get that easy advantage. You might be assumed to be incompetent until you prove you are competent. Tall people are more likely to be pushing an open door. Short people find themselves having to demonstrate their abilities more often and more consistently with a different measuring stick.

Without more tools to use to ensure inclusion and equity, the very diversity we say we want can actually cause more problems than homogeneity, which is less compelling but easier to maneuver. For example, many held beliefs—and continue to hold them—about what

---

[1] Malcom Gladwell, *Blink: The Power of Thinking Without Thinking* (Little, Brown & Co. 2005).

roles are acceptable and proper for women to play and what roles men should play. The bulk of caregiving and housework globally falls to women and, while that is changing somewhat, men play a much less equal role in care and housework. Some countries have strict laws and cultural norms about these gendered roles. Equality Now, an organization that tracks laws that discriminate against women, found in 2020, for example, that "in 59 countries there are no laws on sexual harassment in the workplace, and in 18 countries husbands are legally allowed to prevent their wives from working. Meanwhile, 104 countries have laws that prevent women from working in specific jobs, according to U.N. Women."[2]

How and where we form beliefs about other people was also explored in *The Loudest Duck*. All of the ways we learn about people, I called Grandma (society). Thus, we are all diverse and we all unconsciously bring our Grandmas to work with us.

We learn in myriad ways. Our parents teach us, peers put pressure on us, our everyday experiences in life shape us, religion sends messages to us, and the media, TV, film, and social media are playing a bigger and bigger role in how we learn about others. And all those fairy tales, fables, and myths? Those are strong molders of the archetypes we have of others.

---

[2]"Governments Called On To End Laws That Explicitly Discriminate Against Women And Girls," Equality Now, March 8, 2020, https://www.equalitynow.org/press_beijing25_mar_2020.

I reflected on the great myth of the hero's journey. It is about the young man who has to overcome great odds, slay the dragon, and defeat the evil empire. It looks like he is going to lose to the enemy, but he comes back stronger and overcomes the struggles. He returns to his kingdom, village, or tribe and gets his rewards, which are generally the keys to the kingdom, the pot of gold, and the hand of the fair maiden.

These myths find their way into movies and television. I once read a review of a forgotten, money-losing 2005 movie called *Sahara*, directed by Breck Eisner and starring Matthew McConaughey as "an aquatic treasure hunter who halts a worldwide plague, defeats the evil dictator of Mali, locates a fortune in gold and rolls around a pristine beach in the arms of a scientist played by Penelope Cruz." (At least the woman has a career!)

An equally strong mirror myth is the rescue or rescue me myth. The classic is Cinderella, who is rescued from the evil stepmother by the prince, or Sleeping Beauty who, after lying on a table for 100 years, is awakened by the prince with a (nonconsensual) kiss.

We learn about people unconsciously in so many ways. Movies, fairy tales, and myths depict various archetypes, including the mentor (think Yoda), the orphan (Harry Potter), and the jester or joker (kings often had one to humorously tell them bad news). Generally speaking, men are agents of change and women are waiting to be cared for. Lately, we are seeing more of a mixing in gender, such as Wonder Woman as the hero, but the overwhelming images and archetypes are based on gendered roles. Today, the diversity movement continues to advance, aided by those who understand the moral reasons for change, spurred on by continuing research into the value of diverse organizations, pushed by social justice movements, forced by legal dictates.

Much has changed and yet progress has not been as manifest in the diversity world as it should be, given all of the noise made and efforts that organizations have tried. Diversity has now expanded to diversity, equity, and inclusion, commonly referred to as DEI. It also embraces social justice in its broadened aperture. I have no doubt that 10 years from now there will be further expansion of our understanding and embrace of these concepts.

Unconscious bias training has been seen as an essential part of changing people's mindsets about what views they harbor about others who are different than they are. In my perspective, unconscious bias training has been a ground-shifting exercise, but has not completed the effort. This training must be added onto with actual practical tools for behavior change, for means to de-bias both thinking and processes. Awareness does not necessarily lead to shifts in our behaviors.

I remember why I first started thinking about diversity efforts. It began with my interest in women world leaders and a journey to meet and interview women presidents and prime ministers. These interviews were spurred on by the question of what it would take and what it would be like to have a woman president in the United States (as of 2021, still an unanswered question).

After this journey, having met all 15 of the women presidents and prime ministers of the time period between 1993 and 1996, I co-founded the Council of Women World Leaders, which was originally located at the John F. Kennedy School of Government at Harvard University. Every day on my way to the office I would walk by a park dedicated to JFK, where a memorial features a quote etched in stone from Kennedy's 1961 farewell speech to Massachusetts:

> When at some future date the high court of history sits in judgment of each one of us, our success or failure in whatever office you hold, will be measured by the answers to four questions:
>   Were we truly men of courage. . .?
>   Were we truly men of dedication. . .?
>   Were we truly men of integrity. . .?
>   Were we truly men of judgment. . .?

I'd read that every day and think, "Such good questions to ask men." But of course, they were good questions to ask women too. That was the start of an eye-opening look at how men live in the world and how women go through life. It expanded into thinking about dominant groups and nondominant groups and how dynamics in organizations can cause real problems for those who are not in that dominant group.

The title of the book *The Loudest Duck* refers to how easy it is for some to be under-heard and some to be over-heard and how that can defeat the true essence of a diverse population. In some cultures, people are taught that "the squeaky wheel gets the grease." Speak up and you get what you want. American men often exhibit this culturally learned behavior and it is acceptable for them to do this because Grandma has taught them it is okay. I call this the Wheel.

While doing sessions in Japan, I asked who knew what that squeaky wheel phrase meant. No one knew. They had been taught by Grandma that "the nail that sticks out gets hit on the head." That's 180 degrees away from the squeaky wheel! I call this the Nail.

Another example: women in many cultures have heard the phrase "If you can't say anything nice, don't say anything at all," mimicking the notion that women must above all else be nonconfrontational, nurturing, and unable or unwilling to exhibit anger. Again, 180 degrees opposite of the squeaky wheel. I call this Nice.

Finally, in China the societal norm is "the loudest duck gets shot." Yet another 180 degrees opposite of the squeaky wheel. For example, in some societies' culture it is dangerous to share your political views if they are in opposition to those in power, so not speaking up can seem the smarter approach. In other places, it is considered bad form to ask questions in the classroom because that implies you are questioning the teacher's abilities rather than a simple request for information. I call this the Duck.

So, let's hypothesize that you are in a meeting and the team is diverse because you hired for diversity. It has a Wheel, Nail, Duck, and Nice. Who's likely doing most of the talking? The Wheel, because that is what they have been taught. But looking at it through the lens of cognitive ideas, the group is over-hearing the Wheel and under-hearing the Nail, Duck, and Nice. And the Wheel maybe gets more promotions or assignments or is seen as more valuable because they are the most often heard.

To put this in research terms, multinational professional services firm PWC has found that in a typical eight-person team meeting, on average only three people do 70% of the talking. Organizations need to level the playing field so everyone is heard. I liken it to being a traffic cop (which I was once). The manager of the meeting says, "Let's hear from Jennifer first. Hold on, Bob. Now Andre, what do you have to say? Hold on, Bob." The thing about having a diverse work group means that we need additional tools to make sure the heterogeneous Grandmas are not causing the advantaging of one group over another, of some groups being over-heard and others under-heard, which is the exact opposite of why we wanted diversity in the first place. If we wanted cognitive differing perspectives, we didn't get it.

In this book you will read about the division of responsibility required for ensuring the equitable and inclusive organization that many say they strive for. This is referred to as the Seed and the Soil. The Seed is the individual who has a 50% responsibility for ensuring their career goes well. The Soil is the institution and the management and leadership that comprise the institution, which has a 50% responsibility to bring the necessary tools to bear to create a fair organization. Each manager and leader must act so that their collective action provides the impetus of the organization to overcome systemic problems.

In *The Loudest Duck*, there are two dynamics I see over and over again. One is the lack of real, critical, and actionable feedback for women and other underrepresented groups by those in charge of giving feedback. It may well be a concern for how they will take the critical feedback or a worry that it will be perceived as biased. Sometimes the feedback comes in an unhelpful form. I've seen feedback that tells women to have more gravitas, for a Black person to stop appearing so angry, for an Asian man to be more athletic. None of this is helpful to the person receiving the feedback. I consider the absence of clear, detailed, nonbiased feedback to be one of the major roadblocks to the development of diverse groups. The Soil (organizations and managers) needs to be far more diligent in the processes of giving (and getting) this important development information.

The second dynamic is that some people are good at stating accomplishments, much like they are comfortable speaking up. Others have been taught by Grandma to be humble, not to brag, or to think that their work speaks for itself (hint: your work does not speak; only you do). Worse, some are delusional, thinking a manager will know what they are doing. The disadvantage can be huge, particularly if managers rely on their gut feeling or intuition based on the bragger's statements. The non-bragger is seriously disadvantaged. The Seed (the individual) needs to learn more ways to ensure their work is recognized. They may need to tell Grandma to go home, to get out of their comfort zone, and to speak up more. The Soil needs to solicit the information about what the quiet ones are doing.

One of the tools I recommend is what I call "three up and three down," the purpose of which is to eliminate the effect of the differing Grandmas. The employee expresses to the manager the three things they are doing well, and the manager shares the three things the employee needs to work on. Everyone thereby states accomplishments, and everyone gets feedback. This should happen at least every three months or sooner and can be informal in nature and quick to do. If a manager wants to reaffirm three ways the employee is doing well, that's fine, but they must give three actionable observations of feedback to help develop the individual. It is a simple yet effective tool and it can help de-bias the system instead of defaulting to the unconscious ways people behave.

We have unconscious biases against some and unconscious biases toward others. (The latter looks like "He reminds me of me when I was young.") But I never liked the term "bias." Many people hear both accusation and wrongdoing in that word and it shuts us down to learning more. I have done diversity sessions for thousands of people globally, and I am confident that unconscious bias is an approach that is quite limiting.

My idea is that we have unconscious beliefs, perspectives, perceptions, associations, actions, roles, and archetypes. We need to go beyond unconscious bias, which feels like a limited way of thinking about our own thinking. The unconscious bias training may be necessary, but it is not sufficient. Some critics have assailed the framework because it can be seen as our having thoughts that are beyond our control. If all of this is unconscious, how am I supposed to know that I am thinking this way? How do I know that I am reacting in a hyper-fast way and subtly or not subtly putting people in categories if it is all unconscious?

Others may embrace the beliefs but then cry out, "What do I do once I know what I didn't know before? Give me the tools to help me overcome these harmful beliefs." I did receive feedback that *The Loudest Duck* book helped change attitudes and provided a useful framework and vocabulary to move beyond what diversity had been seen as.

Over the course of August and September 2021, I interviewed scholars, diversity consultants and practitioners, and executive leaders, by phone or, as appropriate for the times, by Zoom. The individuals I cite in this book are world-class thinkers on issues of diversity, equity, and inclusion for whom I have great respect. Either through their leadership of organizations or through their consulting and research, they have advanced the understanding of how we can value and advance these goals.

My hope is that this book will build on *The Loudest Duck* and fill the gap between awareness and action. I hope it will provide a way to move beyond simply a desired outcome to make the goals of a diverse workplace a reality and a win-win for all. Wherever you are on the journey of diversity, equity, and inclusion, the Elephant and Mouse will help you move even further along.

Chapter 1

Hard Truths

WHAT ARE THE HARD TRUTHS ABOUT DIVERSITY, EQUITY, AND INCLUSION?

Let's be realistic as we think about both the successes and failures of the efforts around diversity, equity, and inclusion (DEI). Some say that the whole push toward diversity began at least 20 years ago; others date it to the 1960s. Historians might suggest anti-slavery movements or suffrage efforts were the origins of the impetus for diversity. In any case, it could be argued that this effort has been a long time incubating. We need to acknowledge that although there has been progress, perhaps efforts are not going as well as we would have hoped. Billions of dollars in training, millions of people-hours taking trainings, uncountable numbers of words spoken and written have advanced this desired goal of embracing a diverse, equitable, and inclusive workplace and society. Annual reports, declarations, lawsuits, committees, meetings, articles, and reporters' efforts have helped contribute to the goal of moving the needle.

So what can we show for all of this human energy and lost trees? I would like to stipulate that progress has occurred.

3

But the stipulation is limited. We can look at emerging laws, admissions to military academies or law schools, jobs that women are now in, awareness of issues that face people of color—these all show telltale signs of progress over the past decades.

The evolution of the Barbie doll is as good a metric as any for measuring progress for women. Barbie, the doll, emerged in the late 1950s through the creative imagination of Ruth Handler, who founded Mattel Inc. Ruth wanted girls to imagine futures for themselves. Initially that future looked like a White, thin model, maybe a flight attendant, with feet permanently in the high-heel position. It was a vision of perfection that matched almost no one but certainly created a false sense of beauty. And she had her opposite in the Ken doll, quaffed, White, and (to me, at least) always looking slightly gay, though I doubt Ruth wanted that image at the time. Barbie has now evolved into the doctor, the scientist, the Olympiad. She is Hispanic, Latinx, Black, slightly more zaftig, but not yet Asian. Over 60 years, Barbie has adapted to the times.

Yet milestones continue to weigh down our imagination; canards of beliefs remain prevalent, but they can be changed with effort. For example, in the early 1900s women couldn't easily become doctors and it was believed they didn't want to be; now 50% of doctors are women. Today we continue to have old ways of thinking about who people are and what they are capable of. DEI can help us expand our imaginations even further.

We do need to acknowledge some hard truths as we scan the horizon of change and progress for diversity. We are definitely not there yet, and the rate of progress is not comforting. The World Economic Forum *Global Gender Gap Report* keeps pushing back the number of years until true equality will be seen between men and women globally. It used to be 75 years, then it went to about 135 years.[1] Progress has certainly been made, according to the report, particularly in health and education gaps. But political and economic gaps remain stubbornly high.

In the largest 500 global companies, the number of women CEOs went from 14 women, or 2.8%, in 2020 to what was applauded when the numbers "roared," according to *Fortune*, to 23 women, or 4.6% in 2021 (with 1 and 6 women of color, respectively).[2] To me the notion that a 1.8% increase was roaring forward seems slightly hyperbolic. The push to get women into the C-suite has been around for a long time. Noting the progress seems reasonable, but to celebrate at this point seems overly dramatic.

---

[1] *Global Gender Gap Report*, March 31, 2021, World Economic Forum, https://www.weforum.org/reports/ab6795a1-960c-42b2-b3d5-587eccda6023.

[2] Emma Hinchliffe, "The Number of Women Running Global 500 Businesses Soars to an All-Time High," *Fortune*, August 2, 2021, https://fortune.com/2021/08/02/female-ceos-global-500-fortune-500-cvs-karen-lynch-ping-an-jessica-tan/.

BUILDING AWARENESS

It turns out that the building awareness phase of implementing DEI is just that: awareness but less focus on actual behavior change. Unconscious bias trainings have had mixed results, with a growing realization that the training may not accomplish the goals that were deemed possible. Some who got the training became less amenable to supporting the notions of diversity as a good thing. One could—and many did—walk away thinking that if all this was unconscious, how were they to actually stop negative reactions to others from happening. If my unconscious rejects the "other," how is my conscious supposed to override that intuitive reaction?

Others came away understanding that there are beliefs and archetypes but they did not know how to override them, and the trainings did not provide real solutions to everyday interactions.

Bottom line, the Hard Truth is that these unconscious bias trainings did not move the cause of DEI forward in proportion to the effort, the people-hours dedicated to them, and the money paid for them.

In my 2021 Zoom interview with Kendall Wright, CEO of Entelechy and author of the book *Leadership Soul*, he spoke to this Hard Truth brilliantly when discussing with me unconscious bias. "I don't know that we are ready, even capable of getting past the unconscious bias hurdle. I think that the more we learn, as far as the neuroscience is concerned regarding how bias works, how it operates, and what it safeguards—that sense of threat and loss, I think is a hurdle that had yet to be overcome. And yes, there are a lot of people talking about unconscious bias. But they're talking about it in a way that doesn't necessarily encourage the learner to take ownership for their bias and to be proactive in wanting to identify the bias and then work to manage it."

I can see that the bias will never go away; it's part of how we are hardwired. But that doesn't mean that we have to become prisoners to that hardwiring. All of this frontal cortex that we've been blessed with is there for a reason. And we get to make choices. So the challenge is to understand the unconscious bias and how it manifests in practically every decision that we make, because wherever there is an opportunity for a subjective assessment or analysis you will also find the opportunity for unconscious bias to influence that decision. Too many leaders believe that because they have deemed themselves to have good hearts, they are free of the consequences of the unconscious bias.

FEELINGS OF TAKE AWAY

Some people have a fixed idea that only the best make it and if you try hard enough, you too can succeed. They believe that laziness, lack of will, and poor education are the gatekeepers to making it in the world. Tinker with that basic premise and you disrupt the way the world works and should work. According to this belief system, an individual's success is based on an individual's efforts, so what they earned is now being taken away from them. Individuals experience the world on the individual level; rarely are we able to comprehend that some face extra hurdles that others do not encounter.

I always thought the 1983 Eddie Murphy comedy *Trading Places*, directed by John Landis, was as good a representation of what happens when we are put in situations that disadvantage or advantage, having nothing to do with our own efforts. Dan Ackroyd's character was a White, wealthy broker with a girlfriend, manservant, and mansion. Eddie Murphy's character was a poor, Black street hustler. On a bet by others, they ended up trading places with each other. The story line focused on how they fared, and the ways each ended up adapting to his new and arbitrary assignment of advantage/disadvantage showed how random our likelihood for success in life can be. The Hard Truth is that this presupposes that in fact the world is fair and the ingredients for success are available to all and handed out in a deserving and meritocratic manner rather, than through random bursts of fate.

Change will *not* occur naturally. It is hard to imagine any change that was not caused by something, whether human effort or forces of nature. Little in life remains static; everything has forces pushing or pulling. The Hard Truth is that as, Frederick Douglass said in 1857, "If there is no struggle, there is no progress."[3] To wait and let some mysterious outside force make the societal change with little sacrifice or act of intention is the path to low expectation and even less result. Unlike safety, where everyone benefits in obvious ways, unless organizations make the value of diversity clear, obvious, and unquestioning, the lack of diversity hurts the least powerful the most and requires change from those who are least likely to want to change.

Programs and more programs lead to fatigue and annoyance. The Hard Truth is that the rule of unintended consequences comes into play when organizations have programs but lack strategy and measurable actions. I worked with a company that had embraced an encyclopedia of diversity efforts, from donating money to a Black dance troupe, to funding scholarships for young diverse engineers, to paying large sums to support the employee resource groups.

Training was ubiquitous and mandatory and yet, for all the efforts, there was little closing of gaps amongst the minority and women employees' perception of the company and the dominant group's beliefs. For some, the drumbeat of programs implies that more is being done for minority groups than for those historically in power. This leads to disillusion, fatigue, and annoyance. A good example of annoyance is when a man now says to a woman,

---

[3] Frederick Douglass, 1857, https://shec.ashp.cuny.edu/items/show/1245.

"I'd like to compliment you on your suit, but I'm afraid you will sue me for sexual harassment," or proclaims that he doesn't want to travel with a younger woman for business or mentor her, because he could be exposed to liability. (The antidote to that worry is to suggest acting professionally.)

In the introduction to this book, I reference the concept of "safety first." What that means in most organizations that put a premium on safety is that safety violations are handled clearly and forcefully, either internally or externally. The restaurant with the rats gets shut down, the airplane with the faulty wiring gets grounded, a hazardous work floor gets a fine. What is the equivalent for those who do not engage in diverse best practices or subtly undermine efforts? The Hard Truth requires a doubling down of strategic effort, not just adding to the plethora of programs.

The Hard Truth is that we have two options. Option A is to continue doing what we are doing. Option B is to double down on efforts, make it non-negotiable, and treat the mission of DEI as you would any other crucial mission. I'd like to think most of us are going to choose Option B.

We know that diversity itself is not enough. There can be "the illusion of inclusion," as Cheryl Kaiser describes it.[4] The Hard Truth is that no matter whether you are a

---

[4] Cheryl Kaiser et al., "Presumed Fair: Ironic Effects of Organizational Diversity Structures." *Journal of Personality and Social Psychology* 104 (3): 504–519, https://doi.org/10.1037/a0030838.

corporation, government agency, nonprofit, white collar, blue collar, global, national, local, or small or large in size, diversity, equity, and inclusion is now, and into the future, a key factor for survival and success.

In being asked about diversity progress these past 10 years, I humorously relate a purported conversation between John Major, former prime minister of Great Britain, and Boris Yeltsin, then prime minister of Russia. Major asks Yeltsin, "Tell me in one word, how it's going in Russia." Yeltsin responds, "Good." Major is slightly taken aback given Russia's many problems and says, "Boris, please elaborate; tell me in two words how it is going in Russia." Yeltsin responds, "Not good." That's my answer to how it's going with diversity efforts. Good and not good.

Progress has been made. We see organizations decrying discrimination and protesting loudly that they have programs in place. Women have progressed in many countries, with appointment of a small percentage of women CEOs, women on boards of directors, women in the military ranks and even in combat, Dalits in India being elected to office, and government ministers of African descent in places such as France. Same-sex marriage has been legalized in some countries. Police behavior is under far more scrutiny than in the past in relation to treatment of Black people in the U.S. and those of African descent in other countries.

In 1996, women in the U.S. held 10% of executive positions. In 2021 this has risen to 20%. All Fortune 500 boards have at least one woman.[5] However, many small firms still have no women or minorities.

Beth Brooke, former vice chair of EY, said in my 2021 interview, "I think we're at risk of going backwards at any moment. I don't think women's leadership is particularly valued in the way that I think it's had an impact. Women leaders lead differently, they talk differently—and they're better. Now maybe that's because I'm a woman, but I like their style. I think they're really smart. I think they're not prone to the blinders that men tend to be prone to. But yet, I don't feel like the world sees that at all. I don't think there's any conversation at all. I don't think that women leaders who are doing a really outstanding job are getting noticed."

That said, there are many signs that people, countries, and organizations have responded to the growing voice and demands for focus on visible inequities along with economic or other injustices. One circuit breaker that has emerged robustly in the last 10 years is the quota or affirmative mechanism tool. In some form, 130 countries have electoral quotas to increase the number of women in elected offices.[6] While controversial in some circles,

---

[5] Courtney Connley, "For the First Time in over 20 Years, All S&P 500 Boards Have at Least One Woman," CNBC, December 15, 2020, https://www.cnbc.com/2020/12/15/all-sp-500-boards-have-at-least-1-woman-first-time-in-over-20-years.html.

[6] Gender Quotas Database, International IDEA, 2021, https://www.idea.int/data-tools/data/gender-quotas/country-overview.

no tool has shown the immediacy of results that these affirmative mechanisms have.

Some countries now mandate percentages for women on boards, or in the executive C-suite. Research indicates that because of these efforts there are often more comprehensive solutions to issues, that different voices reflect different experiences and therefore allow for better solutions. What has been shown is that in-group favoritism and closed social networks, which are drivers of homogeneity, do lessen in impact. We see that adding people to the table does not deprive those who have always been at the table. The expanded pool expands opportunities for all.

Corporations now understand that allegations and proof of sexual misconduct can harm them and pose ethical, reputational, and financial risks that affect their bottom line, stock price, and hiring ability. Larry Fink, CEO of global investment firm BlackRock, sent a letter to clients worldwide that highlighted the need to look beyond financial results. Every company must demonstrate how it "makes a positive contribution to society," he wrote, including in diversity and talent management.[7]

---

[7] Laura Liswood, "To Hope or Doubt? The State of Women's Progress in the World," World Economic Forum, December 20, 2018, https://www.weforum.org/agenda/2018/12/women-progress-world-gender-gap-2018/.

WHY GIVING WOMEN A SEAT AT THE TABLE PAYS OFF

Women are good for business. Research conducted over three decades shows a correlation between women's representation in leadership roles and positive outcomes in organizations. Catalyst, Credit Suisse, and McKinsey & Co. have all reported that companies with more women in leadership and on boards have a higher correlation of profitability and financial performance. They also have fewer instances of fraud, corruption, and financial reporting mistakes. It may just be that well-run companies that are more diverse are more profitable, but it certainly points directionally to the value of diversity.

Experience in Norway, which requires companies to reserve at least 40% of board seats for women, has shown that women are more likely to consider the long term, and include constituents other than shareholders in their board deliberations.[8] Women encourage boards to focus more on communities, the environment, and employees.

Women also introduce different legislation into parliaments and deliberating bodies than men do, often related to family, education, and healthcare. With a critical mass in parliament, women can change its hours of operation

[8] "Ten Years on from Norway's Quota for Women on Corporate Boards," *Economist*, February 17, 2018, https://www.economist.com/business/2018/02/17/ten-years-on-from-norways-quota-for-women-on-corporate-boards.

to reflect the needs of legislators with children. In Sweden, proceedings now end at 6pm instead of 10pm. And in a virtuous circle, more women in public office inspire younger women to follow in their footsteps.[9]

When women are involved in post-conflict negotiations, peace is more likely to prevail. A peace agreement is 35% more likely to last for at least 15 years when women are involved in the process.[10] More research is needed for cataloging the benefits of other types of diversity beyond gender; the logic should remain correlating the two.

THE "GLASS CLIFF" PHENOMENON

But the arc of progress is not straightforward. The recent *Global Gender Gap Report* says it will take more than 100 years for the gender pay gap to disappear, at the current backsliding rate of progress.[11] The world is leaving around $12 trillion in GDP on the table because of this gender gap.[12]

---

[9] Liswood, "To Hope or Doubt?"

[10] UN Women 2015, "Women's Participation and a Better Understanding of the Political," A Global Study on the Implementation of United Nations Security Council resolution 1325, https://wps.unwomen.org/participation/.

[11] World Economic Forum Global Gender Gap Report.

[12] "How Advancing Women's Equality Can Add $12 Trillion to Global Growth," McKinsey & Company, September 1, 2015, https://www.mckinsey.com/featured-insights/employment-and-growth/how-advancing-womens-equality-can-add-12-trillion-to-global-growth.

"Industries must proactively hardwire gender parity in the future of work through effective training, reskilling and upskilling interventions, and tangible job transition pathways, which will be key to narrowing these emerging gender gaps and reversing the trends we are seeing today," says Saadia Zahidi, head of the Centre for the New Economy and Society and Member of the Executive Committee at the World Economic Forum.[13]

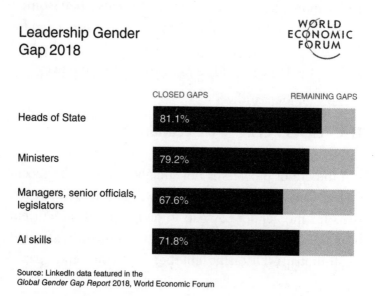

Leadership Gender Gap 2018

WORLD ECONOMIC FORUM

	CLOSED GAPS	REMAINING GAPS
Heads of State	81.1%	
Ministers	79.2%	
Managers, senior officials, legislators	67.6%	
AI skills	71.8%	

Source: LinkedIn data featured in the
Global Gender Gap Report 2018, World Economic Forum

---

[13] "108 Years: Wait for Gender Equality Gets Longer as Women's Share of Workforce, Politics Drops," World Economic Forum, December 18, 2018, https://www.weforum.org/press/2018/12/108-years-wait-for-gender-equality-gets-longer-as-women-s-share-of-workforce-politics-drops/

While the number of women on boards is increasing, it's happening slowly, and often because of government action. In the 44 countries where companies have three or more women on their boards, 43 have government-mandated quotas. Those without affirmative mechanisms are seeing only incremental gains.

Then there is the scrutiny that comes from holding power. Women who make it to the top face a set of challenges unknown to their male peers. They are often perceived as less legitimate. They continue to face unconscious bias, sexual harassment, discrimination, higher expectations, and micro-aggressions—small but steady erosions of their authority.

When women achieve high-level positions, they often face a precipice known as the "glass cliff" phenomenon. They have broken the glass ceiling by rising to leadership roles in dire times, such as financial crisis, controversy, or conflict. Then they are pushed off the cliff if they can't find or create solutions—consider Theresa May and Brexit. As a result, women are often forced out sooner than their male counterparts because of the high-risk nature of their assignments, and the lack of support or authority to accomplish their difficult goals, according to Price Waterhouse Coopers.[14]

---

[14] Liswood, "To Hope or Doubt?"

THE NOT SO GOOD

There is much in the not-good category as well. When it comes to the world of diversity efforts in organizations and with people, I see fatigue, disbelief, cynicism, politicization, efforts that backfire, leaders who speak but don't act, large amounts of misspent energy and money, mixed signals, people feeling like they are singled out, boxes being checked, miscommunication, and useless training. Often, there is a knee-jerk reaction to the scandal-making headlines and a politically correct, albeit insincere campaign for change. All of the usual frameworks of diversity often yield little or slow progress, despite much attention and press given to diversity efforts.

The cynicism about diversity, inclusion, and equity comes not only from those we would like to see embrace the approach and solve unequal treatment, but from those who are often the subject of inequity and unfair treatment. We still hire for difference and fire because they are not the same.

In an article from 2016, Frank Dobbins and Alexandra Kalev show that the millions of dollars spent on programs aren't increasing diversity. Reasons include that managers don't like to be told whom they can and cannot hire. They work around performance systems to reward those they want to, while avoiding diversity blowback. They see mentoring as successful, which increases the mentor's understanding and interaction with diverse groups.[15]

I smile when reading what Joanne Lipman, author of the book *That's What She Said*, declared in a *Time* magazine interview of January 25, 2018. Lipman said that unconscious bias training can heighten biases and people may start walking on eggshells for fear of offending. She says that the most dreaded words said to corporate executives from the human resources department are "We are from the HR department. We are here to help. Now take this mandatory diversity training."[16] For many, this didn't feel like helping at all; it felt like a forced march through nonvoluntary politically correct thinking and confusion about how they were supposed to behave.

The business case for diversity—the benefit, equity, and efficiency arguments that are often given as reasons—do remain true, but if we look at the uneven progress of DEI, they have seemingly not been persuasive. In this book I speak about a different business case for diversity. I think humans are more susceptible to the risk and dangers of doing or not doing something. In Chapter 3, "Beyond the

---

[15] Frank Dobbin and Alexandra Kalev, "Why Diversity Programs Fail," *Harvard Business Review*, July–August 2016, https://hbr.org/2016/07/why-diversity-programs-fail.

[16] Joanne Lipman, "How Diversity Training Infuriates Men and Fails Women," *Time*, January 25, 2018, https://time.com/5118035/diversity-training-infuriates-men-fails-women/.

Business Case for Diversity: Rewards and Risks," I talk about the risk of homogeneity. Homogeneous thinking and groups are much easier to deal with. There is often automatic trust and assumptions of goodwill with a group that is like you. Distrust, different viewpoints, and agendas can cast a shadow and undermine heterogeneous teams. Ironically this is what makes them so much more valuable, but only with more heavy lifting. The heterogeneous groupings *must* have tools, awareness, and processes that help smooth out the inherent differences built into them.

But I do also see hope, progress, continued dedication, good-faith efforts, laws passed, corporations making commitments, and social media pressure to do the right thing. I see governments, tired of slow progress, implement affirmative mechanisms to get organizations to change their behavior more rapidly, to overcome closed social networks and "in" group favoritism. Legal protections have emerged to protect those with disabilities and LGBTQ communities. Stock exchanges and institutional investors pressure companies to move to gender equality at the risk to their bottom line. Societies seek to right racial and gender wrongs. Social movements like MeToo and Black Lives Matter in the 2020 timeframe have emerged as powerful forces. Boycotts, pressure campaigns, and advocacy groups continue to grow and create impact. And yet, as important as these social efforts toward accountability are, they can have unintended consequences. Male managers may be *less* inclined to mentor or sponsor women if they fear that they may make a wrong move and become a target.

I want to continue to help by sharing what I have seen and learned in the last 10 years within the framework of my original effort. The Loudest Duck still holds true (some are over-heard and some under-heard). Noah's Ark is still the motif for many. Grandma continues to teach us and is doing it more powerfully than ever with the social media tools flourishing in recent years. Social media can seemingly broaden our horizons, or it can become an echo chamber of false beliefs and reinforcement of pre-conceived notions.

Amplification and broader reach of ideas are double-edged swords. We can share stories of Indigenous people saving rain forests and we can join extreme groups that have racist views. Who we think people are or should be can be reinforced or altered much more quickly with widespread access to facts and fiction. As technology expands, we can choose to cling to our hardened beliefs, reinforcing those through selective choice of what we hear or read, or take the opportunity to have our world-views altered by new learning and broadened horizons.

THE MODEL T VERSUS THE TESLA

Another force aided by technology is the continuing customization on many fronts. When the car was first invented you had your choice of a black Model T or a black Model T. Today, the number of car styles has proliferated to match consumer demand for almost any car you can dream of. As of this writing, there are 1.8 million Apple apps, appealing to each individual's interests, concerns, or tastes. Not so long ago, TV had three stations. Now think of the myriad niches for diverse viewers with a multiplicity of backgrounds.

In talking about the proliferation of media formats, Laura Grindstaff, a professor of sociology at UC Davis, wrote, "I think for a lot of marginalized groups who've never had their stories told in the mainstream, the atomization has been pretty affirming. Because what kinds of stories were we getting when there just were a few big (movie and TV) hits? Too many that were interesting just to straight, White males."[17]

Now think about the business world, which is playing catchup in understanding that their employees are not monolithic in their needs, skills, lived experiences, and backgrounds. The catchup extends to having programs that fit this burgeoning realization that the straight, White male may experience the organization differently than the transgender female. It certainly extends to requiring leaders and managers to better understand those who are different than they are.

---

[17] Laura Grindstaff, "The TV Hit Isn't Just Dying—It May Already Be Dead," *Washington Post*, June 22, 2021, https://www.washington-post.com/business/2021/06/22/tv-hit-isnt-just-dying-its-already-dead/.

Customization has come to the people in the organizations, much like it has already come to meeting the demands of customers, investors, and governments. It is not that the diversity wasn't already there in many cases, but the voices of the marginalized are more urgently needed to be heard and understood.

Rafael Polanco, senior executive of a financial service company who identifies as Hispanic, said it well in his 2021 interview with me. "People have more need and reason to get into another's shoes. In the workplace, there is now a need to understand what others think, what groups think. Before, you had to fit in. Now it isn't that people are just workers but there are people with differing lives and experiences. Forces outside the workplace are making their way into the workplace, which has also put a spotlight on the imbalances of society."

The need to go deeper and beyond original precepts of diversity seems clear and necessary to me. Awareness and progress have been astounding, but so has the striking lack of progress in the realities and benefits of diversity, equity, and inclusion. It seems that technological progress is certain. Think about the speed of change of computer power and capabilities. But social progress is not as certain. We can seemingly go back to the Middle Ages when it comes to the treatment of certain groups, just as we have the potential to advance.

I also have learned that many seek answers that are action oriented. After having taken unconscious bias trainings, managers and leaders plead for help going beyond awareness to doing something that creates change on an everyday basis.

A significant purpose of this book to follow *The Loudest Duck* is to fill this gap between awareness and action, to provide the tools and upgrade the awareness I believe can hurry history. I want to empower and challenge both the Seed and the Soil in a group. The Seed is the individual who has a responsibility to ensure they are successful in their work and workplace. The Soil is the institution and its environment that allows each seed to thrive and feel a sense of belonging. In my view, each has a 50% responsibility to ensure both individual and institutional well-being.

It is easy to say we embrace principles of fairness or advancement of diversity. It is far harder to shift deeply held habits, entrenched policies, or perhaps even fear of criticism in wanting to change the status quo, particularly if the status quo has always benefited you.

I am not particularly sanguine that we can remove our unconscious biases about others, which are imprinted early on and can continue through what we see and read and what we seek to confirm about what we believe. There is some evidence that this may happen with familiarity and constant reinforcement. In fact, part of this book argues that to move the needle we must develop ways to learn more about other's experiences that are different from our own.

Organizations need metrics, but not just those that measure representation. Pursuing the metrics of the meritocracy gap is one of the most telling mirrors of the differing experiences of dominant and nondominant groups, and will be pursued here, in *The Elephant and Mouse*.

I am convinced organizations can and must de-bias their processes. Otherwise, we are relying on the Tennessee Williams *Streetcar named Desire* strategy, which depends upon the kindness of strangers. We rely upon those who feel engaged and enlightened and when they are gone from the place, the efforts often slow or stop. So we must shift from any one individual's vision or conviction to putting in place ways to ensure that places will sustain these efforts because they are embedded in the DNA of the organization.

The current climate has revised how we must think about leading and being in organizations. Diversity is with us and will continue to be increasingly manifest in societies globally. This inevitability also requires fresh ways of thinking and the replacement of old ways of engaging with our teammates and colleagues. We are now called upon to have humility and curiosity about how others live; to demonstrate sincerity, empathy, and trustworthiness as we interact; to realize that we share the world and its resources in an intertwined way.

Society today is more polarized than ever, it seems. We each have our own window into the world, and it can look very different. That difference can be a roadblock to progress if one group sees a problem and the other does not. The next chapter, on going beyond the Elephant and the Mouse, talks about the "he saw/she saw" phenomenon or any combination of differing worldviews.

I see diversity, equity, and inclusion as strategic tools, as ways to ensure innovation and creativity through different perspectives and cognitive thinking. I want to have a more equitable world and to create a level playing field so all have equal engagement and fair play. But I know that others see loss of centrality, advantaging some over others, positive discrimination phrasing, erosion of a perceived meritocratic system, unfairness, canceling a culture that they value and want to preserve, and disrupting norms that seem fair.

It may never be possible to find common ground, to move to a shared vision, and to meld values. As this book unfolds, as mentioned in the introduction, you will see that I take a page from the Dagoba Group's Mark Kaplan and Mason Donovan. They liken the efforts put into place within organizations to make them safe and accident free to a parallel mindset and focus on DEI. I like this comparison a great deal. We can easily imagine what it takes to have zero defects or safety first, and that same dedication can be applied to the equally essential need to have a fully diverse, equitable, and inclusive workplace.

Chapter 2

The Elephant and the Mouse

The Elephant and the Mouse is a callout to all of us to acknowledge that the concepts and realities of diversity, equity, and inclusion (DEI) are becoming fully embedded in our lives and structures. This requires that we learn more about others, reframe our thinking, overcome our illusions, delve deeper into human behavior, and readjust how we lead.

The fundamental question that diversity efforts expose is what we know about the other and ultimately how we make decisions in the absence or presence of that knowledge. I find this a crucial determinant for creating and implementing successful, diverse, equitable, and inclusive cultures. It is an essential inquiry in looking at those who have dominant roles and those who don't. Presence of knowledge about others does not guarantee success, but absence of knowledge guarantees failure. My metaphor to capture this is the Elephant and Mouse. How much do you know about the other? If you are a member of the group that has traditionally been in power, the other already knows a lot about you.

Historically, out-of-power groups are using social media and other megaphones to make more readily apparent that they do not live in the same world as those that have had the power. They want others to see and recognize differential treatment and places of unfairness. They want understanding that it is possible for the powerful to experience unfairness, but the frequency of those occurrences is far less.

It is my belief that, like the revolution created by the introduction of modern technology, the diversity revolution is forcing individuals and organizations to rethink how they operate at their core, how they act and react, what they believe, and how they think about the world. This is a paradigm shift on the magnitude of the changes required when computers and iPhones and other technologies became both ubiquitous and normal within our workplaces. Technology shifts required learning new skills and replacing old habits. Diversity fully embraced is similarly demanding, particularly because it requires engaging both hearts and minds.

Think about companies that created marketing campaigns that failed because they did not include differing perspectives. For example, "Coolest monkey in the jungle" was printed on a shirt with an accompanying picture of a young Black boy. For some, it immediately harkened back to previous degrading images of Black people as less than human. One has to imagine that if someone who identified as Black had been in the design room, they would have been able to raise a red flag about what would be a most disturbing flashback for some.

Dove is well known for promoting diversity in the beauty industry and is well-intentioned. Through their ads, they have shown that women of various body types—not just the classic thin model—are beautiful. Yet a Facebook campaign created immediate negative blowback because it showed an African American woman changing into a Caucasian woman after using Dove lotion, implying that white was the desired skin color.[1] Chevy denies the urban myth that in Mexico they named a car Nova, which in Spanish means "no go." Kryptonite, makers of the popular and impenetrable U-shaped bike lock, came out with a hefty chain-link lock called "The Noose." Who did they not ask to review these ads? Who was not in the room? Or if in the room, who was not willing to speak up? Or, if they were in the room and spoke up, who did not get heard?

The basic idea of the Elephant and the Mouse is that some people know a lot about other people, and some know very little. In the diversity world, that translates into dominant group members knowing far less about the lived experiences, perspectives, and challenges of those who are not like them. Conversely, by dint of living in a world not made for them, nondominant groups have to learn in any way they can about those who have created much of the structure they live in. Thus, the Mouse knows a lot about the Elephant, while the Elephant knows much

---

[1] Chris Morran, "Dove Apologizes for Thinking Ad Where Black Woman Turns White Was a Good Idea," Consumerist, October 9, 2017, https://consumerist.com/2017/10/09/dove-apologizes-for-thinking-ad-where-black-woman-turns-white-was-a-good-idea/.

less about the Mouse. Survival is one essential and key motivator, and wanting to succeed in a world not structured for them is another reason the Mouse needs to know so much. All diversity, equity, and inclusion efforts will ultimately not succeed to a level desired if this phenomenon of the Elephant and the Mouse remains prevalent.

Unfortunately, we still basically mass-handle people in a corporation. And what I see happening is that people actually want their needs met. So, the Black transgender person says, "These are my needs. I want to be heard, I want to be understood, I want the help with family care." And the LBGTQ person says, "I want to bring my full and authentic self to the workplace and not lose energy, creativity, and belonging if I am hiding who I am." It seems as though we're lagging behind the consumer movement, and I don't think a lot of companies even know how to make that transition.

As Beth Brooke pointed out in her 2021 interview, the COVID-19 pandemic may actually have helped companies start to figure this out, as they consider what the future looks like. "We're watching companies try to deploy, right now, policies around how they're going to bring their workforce back or what kind of hybrid model. And the employees are revolting and saying, 'No we want customization and by the way, if we don't get it here, we'll go get it with our feet—we'll go find our customization; it just may not be with you.'"

The Elephant and Mouse concept can stretch to ideas about large and small nations or large and small corporations. Ask anyone in the world who the president of the United States is and they can almost assuredly name the person. Ask anyone in the United States to name the prime minister of Norway and chances are they will return a blank stare. Similarly, a small startup company in the software business probably knows a lot about the strategy, products, and services of Microsoft; Microsoft may not even realize that the small company even exists.

In *The Loudest Duck*, I shared reflections on Howard Gardner's book *Leading Minds*. Dr. Gardner relates that one of the four traits of great leaders is that they travel outside of their worldview.[2] (The other three are having a true north moral compass, a willingness to challenge authority and the norm, and having the skill to convey your ideas.) Traveling outside of your own worldview is not easy. You need many tools to assist with this and you must have the willingness to go beyond thinking that the world works for others as it works for you, because it does not.

Today it is becoming far more crucial to have empathy, to be curious, to have an open and inquiring mind, and to understand the lived experiences of others through their window. How else can you have successful heterogeneous organizations if you continue to have this knowledge divide?

---

[2] Howard Gardner, *Leading Minds: An Anatomy of Leadership* (Basic Books, 1995).

Both the Elephant and the Mouse bring their own culture into the organization, each culture formed by their own circumstances of life. Every one of us learns how to communicate, how to walk in the world, what we observe, how we react to others, and how we speak. We all have our own point of view and are shaped by experiences and values that are given to us or absorbed by the behaviors of those around us.

I am often amused when I ask what the norm is at family dinner. Have you been told to eat everything on your plate because there are others starving somewhere or because if you leave something it signals you didn't like the food? Or have you been told to leave a little food on your plate to show that the host was not stingy and gave you plenty to eat? If you celebrate Christmas, do you open presents on Christmas Eve or Christmas Day? Are you encouraged to brag about your accomplishments or are you taught to be humble and not toot your own horn? Should you keep a stiff upper lip and not display emotions, or is it better to let everyone know exactly how you feel?

These issues are all directly related to how the Elephant and the Mouse operate in the world. There can be dramatic effects when the two cultures meet, with opportunity for confusion, derision, and impact on success or failure. And it is guaranteed that an organization that embraces diversity will have many cultures coming together (and potentially clashing, being misunderstood, or negatively reacted to unconsciously). Differing cultures have the potential to create differing impacts across what looks like the same policies or processes.

We often hear about women's intuition. This can be explained by the hypervigilance of the nondominant group. Women tend to pay far more attention to men's body language; tone of voice; subtle movements; patterns of behavior; desires, wants, and needs; and key triggers than what men may pay attention to about women. It may be for survival, for peace and harmony, for the desire to be liked and cared for, to feel safe, or for the need to fit in to a world not of their making.

This "knowing" and contrasting lack of knowledge has taken on more urgency as it becomes clear that people are treated in divergent manners because of some category of diversity they reflect. At the same time, the proliferation of video cameras and social media has made it easier to capture disparate or unequal treatment.

Often the minoritized group has to consider much that those who are in the majority don't even realize requires thought. (I discuss this further in Chapter 5, "What You Can Do Easily.") The Elephant walks in the world differently than the Mouse. Each brings their own approach and culture into their everyday lives and into their places of work.

An example of that is the way of speaking or acting in the workplace known as code-switching, which is defined as the act of changing our behaviors, including speech, dress, and mannerisms, to conform to a different cultural norm than what we might authentically do in our own homes.

Persons of color often experience this phenomenon, and it can be exhausting. It is like having to be bilingual, but in the context of societal norms about what are appropriate or acceptable speaking styles in the workplace or in general society. Some groups work hard to reduce their accent at work, only allowing the accent to be more predominant when they are amongst their own group. Ask someone who is of a different diversity category than you if they change their speech patterns when at work versus when at home.

A gay man in one of my discussion groups said he developed quite a good sense of humor early in his life as a defense against being bullied. He carries that with him to work now, but understands that humor too often used may make him appear not serious or less than leader-like. I remember talking to one Black man in an organization about casual Friday dress code. He reflected on the fact that his White male colleagues could "afford" to wear blue jeans on those days without any social consequence. He felt that he would be disadvantaged if he wore jeans or a hoodie, given stereotypes people might hold about him. He said he always wore pressed khakis. His non-Black colleagues might not have had to take that second thought step when they opened their closet on Friday to decide what to wear.

Employees want to feel like their organizations care about them, that they are listened to and understood. As Kendall Wright, told me, "Leaders have to humanize everyone they lead. They have to show real interest in the people who they employ, to ask questions, be curious, understand more about how others live their lives and build trust." Kendall quotes Roxanne Emmerich, who found that leaders who invest in true relationship building saw that their subordinates exert 57% more effort in their work. If you are the Elephant in the room, getting to know the Mouse pays off. People want to be "seen," to be understood, valued, and have confidence that the leaders know what they are going through. Diversity itself is not sufficient. That merely brings many differences into the door. It then becomes paramount that there be effort to ensure inclusion and then to solve for equity.

MEN AND WOMEN: LIVING IN TWO DIFFERENT WORLDS?

I'm often amused by how the Elephant sees the world. Geena Davis, actor and founder of the Institute on Gender and the Media, is doing fascinating work looking at race and gender roles in the media and how stereotypes play out in the media. One study showed that men depicted 62.3% of all STEM characters in movies, while women accounted for 37.1%.[3] Another found that men

---

[3] Geena Davis, "Representations of Women STEM Characters in Media," 2018, Geena Davis Institute on Gender in Media, https://seejane.org/research-informs-empowers/portray-her/.

had three times the speaking roles of women in G-rated movies.[4] I was particularly amused with one study that found that when women were 17% of the participants in a room, men thought women were 50% of the participants. When women were 33% of the room, men saw more than 50%.[5] It is not surprising that men often think more progress has been made than is truly occurring.

As a *New York Times* article revealed, nearly half of men say they did most of the home schooling during the 2020 COVID pandemic; 3% of women say men do that much.[6] In a research study on White men, Chuck Shelton from Diversity Best Practices found that when asked to rate diversity effectiveness among White male leaders in their companies, 45% of the White men gave positive ratings.[7] Among women and people of color leaders, only

---

[4] Stacy L. Smith and Crystal Allene Cook, "Gender Stereotypes: An Analysis of Popular Films and TV," Geena Davis Institute on Gender in Media, 2008, https://seejane.org/wp-content/uploads/GDIGM_Gender_Stereotypes.pdf.

[5] "Casting Call: Hollywood Needs More Women," NPR, June 30, 2013, https://www.npr.org/transcripts/197390707?storyId=197390707.

[6] Claire Cain Miller, "Nearly Half of Men Say They Do Most of the Home Schooling. 3 Percent of Women Agree," *The New York Times*, May 8, 2020, https://www.nytimes.com/2020/05/06/upshot/pandemic-chores-homeschooling-gender.html.

[7] Chuck Shelton, "The Study on White Men Leading Through Diversity and Inclusion," White Men's Leadership Study, February 2013, http://www.whitemensleadershipstudy.com/pdf/WMLS%20Results%20Report.pdf.

21% saw diversity efforts as effective. It may come as a shock, but in the popular movie *Frozen*, which many lauded as a terrific movie showcasing strong women, 59% of the lines were spoken by male characters.[8] (Not to mention that from a body image perspective, those princesses had really tiny waists.) The princess starts out as a person with great power and over time learns how to use it fully. The movie seems to portray that as a threat in need of being controlled. It is unlikely that the girls (and some boys) who embraced the story singing "Let It Go" saw all of this consciously and yet the unconscious lingers below the surface. I *liked* the movie and if it empowered many girls that is wonderful (along with helping boys see women as persons of strength). It is nevertheless hard to shake off those underlying myths and archetypes that we have.

OUR WINDOWS TO THE WORLD

How do you solve a conflict between two parties if one of the parties does not believe there is a problem, or only

---

[8] Jeff Guo, "Researchers Have Found a Major Problem with 'The Little Mermaid' and Other Disney Movies," *The Washington Post*, January 25, 2016, https://www.washingtonpost.com/news/wonk/wp/2016/01/25/researchers-have-discovered-a-major-problem-with-the-little-mermaid-and-other-disney-movies/.

recognizes it as a small issue, while the other party sees a large and continuing problem?

This is no doubt the constant question posed by marriage counselors. And it applies to many other issues, such as climate change, citizen/police interactions, and women's progress. We all have our own lenses through which we see the world. Our window to the world is shaped by experience, hopefulness, unconscious beliefs, and personal filters. The challenge becomes how to reconcile opposing and strongly held beliefs in the interest of improving a situation. As I have written:

> I am constantly intrigued by statistics that show opposing reactions toward women's career progression and gender parity. Catherine Fox, former Corporate Woman columnist for the Australian Financial Review, found that 72% of male senior executives agreed with the statement that much progress had been made towards women's empowerment and career progression. Of the female executives surveyed, 71% disagreed with that statement.[9]

---

[9] Laura Liswood, "To Hope or Doubt? The State of Women's Progress in the World," World Economic Forum, December 20, 2018, https://www.weforum.org/agenda/2018/12/women-progress-world-gender-gap-2018/.

Or consider this:

The Financial Times, in a study last year on Women in
Asset Management, found that 37% of female asset
managers said the situation for women in fund management had improved; 70% of male asset managers
believed the situation had improved.[10] In the same
study, 51% of women in fund management said quotas
would improve matters; 77% of men in fund management said quotas would not improve matters.[11]

In a *Harvard Business Review* article about Harvard
Business School graduates that looked at career expectations between graduating husbands and wives, Dean
Robin Ely found that half of the men thought their career
would take priority.[12] Almost all the women thought their
careers would take equal priority to their husband's. When
asked about major caregiver roles, 75% of the men believed
their wife would take on most of the responsibility; 50% of

---

[10] Chris Newlands and Madison Marriage, "Women in Asset
Management: Battling a Culture of 'Subtle Sexism,'" *The Financial
Times*, November 29, 2014, https://www.ft.com/content/11585c1a-
76ff-11e4-8273-00144feabdc0#axzz3RQWBBxjy.

[11] Liswood, "To Hope or Doubt?"

[12] Robin Ely, "Life and Leadership after HBS," Harvard Business
School's Alumni Survey, May 2015, https://www.hbs.edu/women50/
docs/L_and_L_Survey_2Findings_12final.pdf.

the women thought they would take on most of this type of work. (In reality, 86% of the women took on the major caregiver roles, exceeding men's expectations!)

So what causes this discrepancy of worldview? And who is right? I posed the latter question to Judith Resnik, Arthur Liman Professor of Law at Yale Law School. Her answer was that both men and women are right, at least based on what they are observing and what facts or cues they give weight to for their differing conclusions. Several explanations can be put forward for these differences:

1. Worldviews compare potential versus performance.

    Men assume policy leads to positive impact. Women see that these policies are not leading to positive outcomes. For example, men saw that there was a program to mentor women, which they viewed as an affirmative program to help women's progress. Women saw no results from the mentoring program. For men, it was the potential and the effort that gave them a sense of well-being. For women, their conclusion of dissatisfaction was based on performance.

2. We all experience confirmation bias.

    This is the phenomenon of sorting facts and observations in a way that confirms what we already believe. So, if men think progress is being made for women, they will place more weight on the facts they see and believe that confirm the advancement, and pay less attention to the impact of the impediments. Women will similarly focus more on the facts that confirm lack of progress and less on the advancements.

3. Cui bono?

Who most feels the impact of the unlevel playing field? When it comes to gender issues, some men generally don't feel the impact (this may not include men from historically powerless groups, who certainly can feel the effects). For women, gender issues have full impact, affecting their lives constantly. Our gender identities shape what hurts and helps us, knowingly or unknowingly. We are all right and we are all wrong in our different lenses.

4. We want the same things.

Both men and women are looking for the same thing at work, including compelling colleagues, mutual values, and challenging work. Based on their experiences, men might be more likely to achieve those work goals; women, on the other hand, may have experiences that create a diminished sense of satisfaction. Given these feelings of dissatisfaction in the workplace, women may have a lower threshold when it comes to deciding whether to leave the world of work or not.

From 2020 to 2021 during the COVID pandemic, masks were often required around the world to help contain the spread of the deadly virus. In the United States in mid-2021, the requirements started to relax after many were vaccinated. One small benefit was attributed to mask wearing for women. As Ashley Fetters of the *Washington Post* observed, women (and a few men) didn't have to worry about some random stranger telling them to "smile."[13] They didn't have to concern themselves with rudely hearing from those who had no right to say anything to the women but nevertheless felt entitled to do so, making comments about their bodies or other aspects, much like what happens with street catcalling and unwelcome overtures.

My friends and I discussed this and the husband of one of the women asked his wife if that had ever happened to her. She looked at him in stark amazement, as did all the women, laughingly saying that it happened often to her. This tall handsome man had no idea; he had

---

[13]Ashley Fetters, "Masks Are Off — Which Means Men Will Start Telling Women to 'Smile!' Again," *The Washington Post*, May 22, 2021, https://www.washingtonpost.com/lifestyle/2021/05/22/men-telling-women-smile/.

never experienced that and said that if some unknown man had said that to him, he would have responded aggressively, wanting to hit the verbal intruder. Taking a page from the Chapter 5, "What You Can Do Easily," while a man has the option to react aggressively, a woman would never consider the possibility of responding in an aggressive manner because of the physical danger that could arise.

I suspect that women have so normalized the "honey," "sweetie" catcalling and verbal intrusions as just something to be endured in the normal course of living as a woman in most societies. They may have suppressed their anger and may not even mention it, so the men have no idea this behavior goes on in their own neighborhood.

Because we are all human (see Chapter 6, "We Are All Human, with Help from Nonhumans"), I recommend we may need to add another set of eyes and ears to our workplace processes. Most of us are only dimly aware, if at all, that we have unconscious beliefs that impact how we view the world, how we look at and treat others, and how we ultimately behave.

That's why we need additional players in our workplace, to help ensure we are part of the success of a fully diverse, inclusive, innovative, and equitable organization.

These additional actors or actions can save us from the problematic dynamics of the Elephant and the Mouse. At minimum, they can flag these actions that have come to seem normal but should not be.

We are all human and we bring our Grandmas to work with us. These Grandmas reflect how we were taught to be, who we saw as role models, what we got taught about others, what behavior was rewarded, and what was ridiculed or shamed. From an early age we learned from our parents, peers, teachers, daily interactions and everyday experiences, pictures on the wall, religion, movies, TV, social media, the fables and fairy tales that were read to us at bedtime.

Most of the time we bring our Grandmas to work with us unconsciously, and every culture has different Grandmas. The more diversity we seek or just have, the more varied our Grandmas. The following list illustrates the impact of culture in the workplace through the lens of both the Elephant and the Mouse, with tools to bridge the two ways of being.

If you are the Elephant:

1. Understand how your culture, your team's culture, and the organization's culture come together in the workplace. Develop appreciation for the value that different cultural styles bring.

2. Develop the Mouse's perspective. Respect and appreciate approaches that are different from the dominant culture.

3. Notice how team members' cultural adaptations may unintentionally convey certain messages. We all bring our own culture to work with us.

4. Ensure individuals with different styles are included and have the airspace to express their views and ask questions.

5. Actively demonstrate your interest in learning more about others' culture and how culture shapes behavior and thought.

6. Get in the habit of soliciting one example of accomplishment from each team member on a regular basis.

7. Culture informs communication and meeting style facilitation: Be aware of your team members' natural approaches and encourage them to flex different styles.

8. When you coach team members, be vigilant that coaching terms used may not be known to those of another culture. Phrases such as "having presence," "gravitas," or "command the room" may not easily translate into actionable desired outcomes.

If you are the Mouse:

1. Understand your culture, your manager's culture, and what each brings to the workplace.

2. Be aware of your cultural adaptations and the messages they convey. We all bring our own culture to work with us.

3. List three values you and each team member add through your own cultural experiences, and three values you and your team members could learn from different cultures.

4. Create a dialogue with your manager about your culture and what you learned from it.

5. You have a point of view, an expert opinion, a question that challenges the collective. Get in the habit of sharing it.

6. Grow comfortable with the "I." Once a week in a format your manager favors, provide one example of your accomplishments and one example of your team's.

7. Know your goals, convey them, and have the confidence to achieve them.

8. Flex your communication and meeting style for maximum effectiveness: If you are indirect, note the direct communications on your team and instances where they excel, and vice versa if you are a naturally direct communicator.

9. Ask for clarification if the person giving feedback tells you to have more presence, look more leader-like, or command the room.

10. Ask for feedback about your brand and continue to refine it.

GlobeSmart is a company that helps organizations work across cultures. Their five-part grid captures differing cultural frameworks, roughly characterizing the United States (on the left) and China (on the right). Of course, no culture is monolithic, but they suggest that these are overall directional ways of behaving.

United States	China
Interdependent: Me-focused.	Interdependent: We-focused.
Egalitarianism: Everyone on the team is equal.	Status oriented: The boss is always right.
Risk: Go for it; you hesitate you lose.	Restrained: Don't count your chickens just yet.
Direct speaking: Concise, concrete, explicit.	Indirect Speaking: Opinions, suggestions, implicit.
Task: What have you done for me lately?	Relationship: It's about who you know, not what you know.

In diverse organizations, we fundamentally seek difference and that ironically makes us clumsy and culturally challenged. If we pursue diversity, then we have no choice; we must pursue better ways to embrace and understand our differences. Otherwise, my suggestion is you eschew diversity and stick with homogeneity and its consequences. Why go into a mission if you only go part way? Or why do it, if you are setting yourself up for failure by not thinking through all that is required? The rule of unintended consequences will surely be the result.

We need help to better understand and get along. We need tools and actors that can help us listen, learn, and act to be better. These include:

- The active bystander
- The wing woman/man
- The independent interlocutor or scribe
- The keen observer
- The ally
- The technology

We need others who can reflect on both the Elephant and the Mouse and help us navigate the two.

Each of these actors will be discussed in Chapter 6, "We Are All Human, with Help from Nonhumans," which expands upon the roles and tools that are essential in a diverse organization where knowledge about each other is lopsided and often power derived.

There is another important aspect to the Elephant and the Mouse. I believe that we are best when we can be flexible and respond to situations based on the nature of the situation itself. Those of us who have the most ways of responding are likely to be most successful. In leadership theory, this is often referred to as "situational" leadership style. (I discuss this more in Chapter 7, "The Elephant and Mouse Inclusive Leader.")

My belief is that both the Elephant and the Mouse offer instructions on how to be in the world. To start, the

Elephant pretty much goes where it wants to go and is seemingly less concerned about what others think or do because it feels a primacy of being. It trumpets loudly and without edit, focused on what it has to say rather than the impact it might have on others. It seldom appears in doubt or lacking in any sense of self. If there is conflict, the Elephant feels confident it will be victorious, rarely doubting its abilities.

The Mouse has developed some strong skills in look-ing out for the "other." It has to be concerned about what the other thinks; it has to hone its telepathic sense with a strong awareness of, if not empathy for, the other. The Mouse can be quite sure it knows a lot about those in its orbit if for no other reason than to get along, outwit, or to be in harmony. Conflict is not its friend. The Mouse develops creative ways to multitask. It can eat and still keep an eye out on what the Elephant is doing. For me, the best use of the traits of both Elephant and Mouse are when they are called upon and when the action fits the moment. Each has a perspective born of their lived expe-riences and each can teach the other.

Here is an interesting footnote to think about. In some fables, the Elephant is often scared by the Mouse because it doesn't know what harm it might do and because it has never had to confront this small, rapidly moving rodent. Not to stretch the analogy too far, but sometimes we observe that people in power are actually afraid of those who are different than they are. They are worried about how the power balance may shift and what the implications are for them. Will they lose power or lose being the central figure in society? Will they have to acknowledge and accommodate others and feel the forces of change upon them? What happens if those who were treated badly when out of power get into power? Will they then treat others the way they were treated? These types of fears can create backlash or resistance to changes in the status quo or to go back to the way things were "before."

Each of the chapters in this book have elements of Elephant and Mouse in them because we all come to the workplace (and life) with ourselves. We do this both consciously and unconsciously, and it can have a direct impact on whether the goals of diversity, equity, and inclusion are ever truly met.

Chapter 3

Beyond the Business Case for Diversity: Rewards and Risks

Many articles, speeches, and conferences focus on the business case for diversity and why organizations should think about the positive rationale and benefit for embracing DEI (and now DEI plus J, which is social justice). Let's look again at why.

REWARDS

Morally, it is the right and ethical thing to do. Everyone is entitled to a fair workplace and an opportunity to succeed without prejudice or bias or preconceived notions of who they are. Diversity can improve the corporate culture by ensuring that people who are part of the team feel empowered, accepted, welcomed, and that their ideas matter. It is not morally acceptable to be found to be lacking in fairness.

Diversity is not limited to initiatives and notoriety in the United States. Many organizations around the world are global in nature, thus having built-in diversity and, at minimum, culturally diverse groups. They have to understand

and embrace these differences by nature of the places they work. Think of an American company with a large presence of Japanese colleagues and regional offices in Frankfurt and Lima. Imagine a Dutch company whose product is sold worldwide and manufactured in lower-cost countries. If its board of directors and its senior leadership is all Dutch, it is highly likely they will make errors in their dealings with the other countries' compatriots. One executive in Frankfurt for a large multinational company, headquartered in America, told me that he was fairly certain he could rise in the organization to lead the Frankfurt office. He had no clear path, however, to taking on more senior roles in the American headquarters.

The law requires diversity. Many countries have now implemented quotas and laws that prohibit discrimination. In some countries, regulatory bodies such as stock exchanges are pushing (often forcing) companies to have diversity plans, to respond to questions, including the issue of why the companies who are lacking women or diverse groups in leadership or on the board don't remedy the situation. A growing number of countries around the world have legally mandated affirmative mechanisms, such as those begun almost 20 years ago in Norway. That country mandates that 40% of corporate board seats must be of the opposite gender, otherwise the company could be delisted from the Norwegian stock exchange and dissolved.

There may be many who disagree with the quota type mandates, who hold up the spectrum of less than qualified "quota appointments." Some argue that the same few women and minorities keep getting appointed to more boards, even referring to the women as "golden skirts." It turns out that there are few incidences where women are less qualified than men, and it is often more a case of "golden trousers," where the same few men keep getting appointed to lots of boards generally because of in-group favoritism and closed social networks of people who know people. Over those objections to quotas, the mandated representation laws continue to pass in more and more places, whether for parliaments, boards of directors, or executive suites. The laws reflect the stubborn resistance to change and the slow progress of efforts for equity. Many are frustrated with the stickiness of the status quo and seek more powerful circuit breakers to create change.

We understand that perspectives are different based on the lived experience of others, while creativity and innovation rest on this need for varying views. If our world view is different, we are likely to challenge the assumptions of the status quo and more likely to want to disrupt the status quo. All companies need to stay attuned to change, whether in the realm of new technology or new clothing designs. The tools required to ensure that diversity, equity, and inclusion are implemented are precisely the tools that good leaders need to have.

Employees, particularly those from underrepresented groups, want to see others like them where they work. Desirable potential recruits to a firm may be reluctant to

join if they see few people who look like them at the top.
If, however, they do see others who look like them, it
sends a powerful signal that joining that organization will
likely provide opportunities and development.

Demographics are changing. Minority majority pop-
ulations are increasing around the world. If a company
seeks the best and the brightest, then the bigger the pool,
the more likely there are more of the most talented. Note
that I do not reflect upon financial gain. Many studies
have hypotheses that diverse companies or boards will
show better ROI, ROE, or other financial indicators. I
doubt that the consultancies and research studies are
actually wrong in their analysis. It would be comforting to
know that businesses may have a higher ROI if there are
three or more diverse people on a board or in the management committee. However, so far, in my reading of
the studies, the gains are correlative, not causal. In other
words, we can't really prove that diversity alone is the
driver of the financial improvement. Plus, what if companies have a down year? Does that mean they don't really
need diversity anymore? It's a slippery slope argument. It
overlooks the fact that diverse groups, when managed
well, are likely to be better places to work, have more
meritocratic systems for everyone, and acknowledge that
all deserve a fair workplace and ultimately a fairer society.
These well-run companies are likely to stay ahead of their
competitors by being innovative and open to changes in
the environment. It then is not too far of a stretch to

assume that these well-run organizations will have better financial results over time.

What does not get nearly enough daylight in these arguments for the business case is observation and cataloging of the *risks* of not having heterogeneity in a workplace. What if you say the right words, but don't actually implement them properly?

RISKS

There is a risk of homogeneity. This is probably the most obvious problem, but is often overlooked. As Scott E. Page, professor at the University of Michigan and author of *The Difference: How the Power of Diversity Creates Better Groups, Firms, Schools, and Societies*, noticed, "A group of smart people does not make a group smart."

Homogeneity's sister term is "groupthink," and that can get dangerous. Groupthink—wherein people may deceive themselves in the name of preserving harmony or the desire to avoid dissent—can have consequences. It often creates nonoptimal decision-making because there is a psychological desire to conform, or the culture does not view dissent as valuable. Those who potentially see a different viewpoint may remain silent, believing or observing that dissent is impossible, futile, or unwelcome. The premature ending of debate can leave problems unseen or unsolved and may leave more creative ideas unexplored.

Many organizations have been doing fine in their homogeneity of decisions, until they aren't. Homogeneous tendencies leave an organization exposed to a greater possibility of making mistakes or of creating difficulties in the future. Why take the risk?

One suggestion is to assign the role of devil's advocate for major decisions being made. This person (or persons) can play a role that is both accepted and welcomed by the group and can raise the questions or issues that may not have been seen or spoken. This role can assure that groupthink is minimized.

The growing danger of reputational risk buttressed by active social media scrutiny means something. Boycotts, protests, and public shaming are the norm, not the exception anymore. The concept of a company as an island accountable only to shareholders has shifted to the idea of an entity in a glass house with many outsiders willing to throw stones at it. Private sector action and public sector good are no longer separate. The role of the CEO as a voice for social equity has shifted. Companies are expected to take a stand on social issues and many employees want to work for companies that do. But the charge of hypocrisy will stick if their company talks a good game but doesn't demonstrate that same poster child equality.

The danger of risk-oriented behavior is not balanced by risk aversion tendencies. This has a gender/racial component to it; research does show that dominant-group men will embrace more risk in their decision-making because they do not suffer as much if the risk-taking fails. Women and other underrepresented individuals have experienced the hazards of risk behavior and the over-scrutiny around failure that accompanies risk-related decision-making. They come to the table with more risk aversion. The value of diversity is having both lenses equally considered to shape decisions.

More people's opinions count now. Institutional investors, pension funds, and activist shareholders all have taken positions about what companies should look like and how serious they are about ESG (environment, social, and governance) issues. Even lawmakers are weighing in. As mentioned, some countries have legally mandated quotas for women on boards. California has passed legislation requiring that boards with six or more members must have at least three women on their board by the end of 2021.[1]

This is a trend that is likely to continue unabated, reflecting on the slow progress being made to include more non-majority groups. Many executives express dislike for anything that represents a mandated quota. My suggestion to them is that they should act "as if" a quota existed and look at how they would meet it if it was in fact required.

[1] Nicholas Goldberg, "California's Controversial Law Requiring Women on Corporate Boards Is Back in the Crosshairs," *Los Angeles Times*, August 2, 2021, https://www.latimes.com/opinion/story/2021-08-02/california-women-corporate-boards.

Mandates like these come from a sense of frustration that there has been more talk than action; affirmative mechanisms suggested above are a way to overcome those closed social networks and the in-group favoritism of recommending a good friend rather than widening the circle. In other words, just adding a trusted golf buddy whom you know well to your company isn't going to be acceptable. Still, today's board room is about 75% male in the U.S. and U.K., and in some countries there are almost no women or minorities on boards of directors.

Other countries have used various non-quota tools with some success such as proxy disclosures, if not/why not explanations (explaining why you have not named a certain number of women or other diversities to the board), name and shame (publicly naming companies that are not living up to their purported or stated values), and women's lists. The last one includes having ready access to women (and others) who are "board ready" or turning to networks whose members are composed mainly of the targeted groups. The scrutiny about the presence of ethnic or racial minorities is gaining momentum as the results for their representation are even slimmer than for White women.

Boards of directors are also doing more board audits to assess whether they have the diversity of background and talent needed, such as technology expertise, marketing experiences, or understanding of government processes. Term limits, age limits, and the expansion of board seats are tools that boards are using to enhance their efforts to ensure diversity of their members.

In the introduction, I stated the obvious, that the world is getting more complicated. My former Goldman Sachs colleague and Artemis asset manager Kathleen McQuiggan looks at her work and estimates that 90% of a company's value is now seen in intangible assets. Property, plant, and equipment still counts, but so do human capital, goodwill, innovation, diversity, reputation, teamwork, workforce turnover, skills and development training, and ESG scores. Corporate disclosure requirements from securities commissions are increasing in specificity. Where people have the luxury of choice in their work environment, they may choose not to work for organizations that don't meet the test of a good citizen.

The risk of overconfidence in decisions can be problematic. Overconfident people are sure of their decisions, even in the absence of data or counter opinions. I love the statistic that 71% of men believe they are above average.[2] This can lead to risky investing, wasting time on fruitless ideas not tempered by fact, getting into dangerous or hazardous situations (e.g. not asking for directions),

---

[2] Patrick Heck and Christopher Chabris, "65% of Americans believe they are above average in intelligence: Results of two nationally representative surveys," PLOS ONE, 2018, https://www.ncbi.nlm.nih.gov/pmc/articles/PMC6029792/.

and an unwillingness to listen and learn from others. Women are often criticized for being underconfident (a point to be debated), but less criticism or concern seems to fall on the trait that men often exhibit, which is the risk of overconfidence.

Risk of confusing confidence with competence is a corollary to risk of overconfidence. To clarify the difference, confidence is how good you think you are; competence is how good you really are. To quote Tomas Chamorro-Premuzic, "competence is an ability; confidence is a belief in that ability....There is no simple way of determining whether someone's confidence corresponds with his or her abilities unless you can measure the person's abilities. (In one test of this)...results revealed that there is less than a 10 percent overlap between how smart people think they are and how smart they actually are."[3]

We see this overconfidence disguised as competence in people who talk over others, or talk more than their fair share, won't admit to not knowing, demand promotions, and overstate accomplishments. The risk is that the person who boasts about a job well done may get the next promotion over the person who has done a huge project well but doesn't brag about it. We know the double bind

---

[3] Tomas Chamorro-Premuzic, *Why Do So Many Incompetent Men Become Leaders? (And How to Fix It)* (Harvard Business Review Press, 2019).

on this is that women and minorities who appear confident are not liked, while men can be confident and still be liked.

Clients do care, or at least some of them do. This is both reward and risk. The reward is that if you are in the business of satisfying and gaining customers and clients, it makes fundamental sense to respond to their needs. If nobody needs or wants the mousetrap, why build it? The risk is that without a broader perspective, you may not know what the client wants and may miss the targeted market.

I remember one leader who pitched a deal to a company in a competitive situation who was told his team got the job because they were the most diverse team who presented. In this case the head of the client team was also a woman. "We hired you because you brought the most diverse team and we knew you would likely be more attuned to our business," the leader was told. The CEO of the winning team thanked her and then requested that she advise the other bidders that she chose them because they were the most diverse.

Ernst & Young has done research on its client work and found that diverse teams have higher client satisfaction. If the client or customer composition is diverse, they will notice a lack of diversity and react accordingly. That said, just adding a diverse person to a team, without them having a significant and valuable role, will not go well with a client who can see through that ruse (and the employee who sees what is being done to them).

Thucydides said that people change for three reasons; fear, self-interest, or honor (or put another way: pain, gain, or vision). The business case for diversity, equity, inclusion, and social justice embraces all three of the reasons to change.

The "gain" case for diversity hasn't seemed to move the needle as much as many hoped. We do know that humans tend to fear loss more than hope of gain. We are more fearful about losing a dollar than we are hopeful of gaining a dollar.[4] We also know that it takes a long time to develop a reputation for trust. That trust can evaporate in a moment when a company stumbles. Saying you cherish diversity and then doing something hypocritical can be a quick slide downward with an even harder climb back to credibility.

Marques Benton, a Black man senior executive at an investment company says, "Race used to be the third rail, but now the expectation is that organizations will engage in discussion. Some are still skittish, more worried about how to say it, and some see it as a moment of learning and listening."

Some organizations don't even want to dip their toe into diversity waters or get involved in public commentary about issues that reflect on societal norms. Once you

---

[4] David Greene, "Why We Care More About Losses Than Gains," NPR, October 25, 2013, https://www.npr.org/templates/story/story.php?storyId=240685257.

make a statement or publicize too forthrightly you may become more of a target, more subject to the shame of hypocrisy. That may be a temporary strategy, but in the long run you will be playing catchup, possibly with reflexive, knee-jerk actions that lack strong underpinnings of solid thinking.

Making clear what we stand to lose if DEI&J are not part of the way we conduct ourselves becomes an essential part of the equation. We must embrace all of the values that diversity brings to our lives and work, such as the richness of different experiences and perspectives. We should celebrate when people feel treated with equity, dignity, and respect, and should reflect that in their enthusiasm and dedication to their workplace, colleagues, and mission. Concomitantly, we need to have a keen appreciation that much can go wrong as the society we live in evolves and readjusts its thinking, priorities, norms, and beliefs and we do not. Rolling the dice by doing nothing or not doing something well and hoping the dice roll will always favor us is not a long-term strategy. A thoughtful diversity plan that considers the views and experiences of all and is clear-eyed about risks and rewards can lead to a favorable long-term strategy.

Chapter 4

Our Illusions, Myths, and Mindsets

Each of us is a collection of reality, lived experiences, learned knowledge, and our own set of illusions, myths, and mindsets. Many of those illusions, myths, and mindsets occur from a combination of confirmation bias and how we think the world works. Confirmation bias is basically our need to confirm that which we already believe about someone or something. It is not "seeing is believing," but rather "believing is seeing." We give more weight to evidence, impressions, or facts that are consistent with our held beliefs, and attribute less importance and credence to that which is contrary to what we already believe.

Think about what many people assume about women drivers, for example. If someone does something stupid in the car in front of you and you see the driver is a woman, you might think, "Of course there's a woman behind the wheel!" You didn't notice the five men who were responsible for idiotic driving in front of you at other times.

Basically, illusions, myths, and mindsets make up parts of what we believe, some of which may be true, and others are simply an accumulation of what we have heard from others (such as from parents, on social media, or what our religion instructs us). They are what we use to

71

justify how we treat or think about someone, and what gets affirmed or rewarded based on these beliefs.

This chapter will explore several illusions: the myth of meritocracy, the illusion of inclusion, thinking that intent is the same as impact, and the ways we confuse effort with outcome. For example, I have never met a leader in an organization who has admitted, "I got to the top of this company because I was subtly advantaged." Nobody says that. Instead, you often hear, "I got to the top because this is a meritocracy, and only the best make it." This is unfortunately a myth and a mindset. Within every organization there are subtle ways that some people receive advantage and others may be disadvantaged or not given positive efforts to help them prosper in their careers.

Here are some other myths:

I believe in meritocracy and fortunately that's what happens here. We recruit talented people, give them opportunities, and then they earn their promotions and advancement.

As we will see in this book, there are conscious and unconscious gate keepers that speed up or slow down people's success. Among them are assumptions about competency, uneven assignment of jobs and projects, differing levels of feedback, and the human urge to favor those like ourselves.

In one American company we held focus groups with four groups: White American men, women, American minorities, and non-Americans, asking whether they believed the organization was a meritocracy. After viewing the results, I went back to management and said there was some great news. One of the four groups thought the company was a meritocracy! You might be able to figure out which of the groups thought that (White American men). The other three did not experience the same feeling of meritocratic treatment.

Another organization did interviews and found similar results. The majority group, with close to 100% agreement, saw the company as a meritocracy. The women did not, as they felt they did not receive the same resources; the Black employees felt they weren't given the same opportunities to advance; the LGBTQ members did not feel like they could be comfortable as their authentic selves.

> *If people just worked harder, made fewer mistakes, and asked for what they wanted or needed, they would be successful.*

Research has shown that nondominant groups have their mistakes overscrutinized.[1] I remember President

---

[1] Abhishek Parajuli, "The punishment gap: how workplace mistakes hurt women and minorities most," World Economic Forum, June 18, 2019, https://www.weforum.org/agenda/2019/06/the-punishment-gap-how-workplace-mistakes-hurt-women-and-minorities-most/#:~:text=Federal%20civil%20rights%20investigations%20in,mistakes%20are%20exactly%20the%20same.

Vigdís Finnbogadóttir of Iceland, who was the first woman president in the world, telling me that she was never able to make mistakes because the press was quick to point them out. Diverse groups may not be sponsored in ways as often as the dominant groups are. The over-scrutiny of mistakes feeds into the feeling that there might be more risk when sponsoring diverse groups because they might fail more. It becomes a vicious cycle, which ultimately leads to disadvantaging some while advantaging others, just the opposite of a meritocracy.

> *Often when minorities or women complain about an issue that has occurred in the workplace, such as not getting a promotion or assignment, the man or non-minority may think, "Well that's happened to me, so it probably has nothing to do with your being a woman or minority." To take it a step further, some will think, "I reflect that this has also happened to me, but I was able to rise above a particular disadvantaged moment, so you should be able to also," little realizing that it may happen to some only a few times in their life. But others may experience this much more often, regularly and repeatedly. That is often why what we see as a one-off simple mistake or comment is something that another person has heard or experienced frequently and tediously. For example, you might be praised for being very articulate in a speech. To some this seems a compliment and a*

*positive reinforcement. But to some who hear "you
are so articulate" often, it might suggest that the listener is surprised that someone "like you" would be
able to be articulate at all.*

People can confuse a one-time situation that has
happened to them with a multiple and frequent occurrence that happens to others. Kendall Wright, CEO of
Entlechy Training and Development, identifies this as
"possibility and frequency." For example, any one of us
may be searched randomly during airport security
screening. But the men named Mohammed whom I
have asked about this say they are randomly searched 99%
of the time. I may expect to be randomly searched occa-
sionally when I travel, but for Mohammed it is a very
frequent occurrence. Mohammed and I live in different worlds.

So those who have experienced a "sometimes or
one-time roadblock" do not realize that the "one time"
for them is actually a frequent set of experiences for
another. The result is that the one who experiences
something infrequently minimizes the experience of
those for whom these situations are replicated time
and again.

WUSA, a TV station in Washington, D.C., performed
a sting in 2013 in which a White man hailed a cab and
then a Black man hailed a cab. The study found that cab
drivers were "25% less likely to pick up a Black passenger

than a White passenger."[2] (Taxi drivers also disproportionately failed to pick up people with disabilities.) The year before that, the *Los Angeles Times* reported the same dynamic for White and Black men hailing a cab.[3]

The irony is that we can all relate to having a one-time experience of a cab not picking us up. But we don't necessarily know what it is like to have a cab pass you by five times more frequently. I remember a U.S. Department of Justice lawyer who was Black say to me that if he was dressed in a suit with a briefcase, he might try hailing a cab. If he was in jeans, he never even exerted himself to flag a cab, to avoid the frustration and indignity of the situation.

THE MYTH OF MERITOCRACY

According to Linda Hill, a professor at Harvard Business School, "Two people start at the same place upon hiring. One gets regular critical feedback, stretch assignments,

---

[2] Will Wrigley, "WUSA9 Investigation Finds D.C. Cab Drivers Discriminating Against Black Customers," HuffPost, December 6, 2017, https://www.huffpost.com/entry/wusa9-taxi-discrimination-video_n_3326228.

[3] Anne Brown, "Undercover sting by black police officers prompts crackdown on racial bias by LAX cab drivers," *Los Angeles Times*, January 20, 2016, https://www.latimes.com/local/california/la-me-lax-taxis-race-20160120-story.html.

mentoring, and sponsoring, and the other does not. After five years of time, there is a *real* performance difference between the two."

I worked with one financial institution that assigned research to the analysts in their department with the belief that the assigning managers were providing similar opportunities for all. Once we actually looked at who received assignments, it became clear that the male analysts got the large capital manufacturing companies, and the female analysts were given the small to medium capital service companies. Prior to showing the managers these results, they had been confident that assignments were being given out fairly, with everyone receiving equal opportunities.

For an organization, solving this lack of meritocracy starts with awareness that there may be a problem. This may come from anecdotes, surveys, or individual complaints. Next comes moving beyond the anecdote to the collection of data to identify whether, in this case, the assignment process is fair or not. If uneven treatment presents itself in the data, those doing the assignments must be shown the proof. (We are human and tend to believe we are fair, but many don't realize what is actually happening.) Processes must change with the input of the assignors and the assigned. Included in the possibility of change may be the use of data analytics or algorithms that remove some of the discretion being applied unevenly. Ongoing evaluation is then essential to ensure that the effort creates the desired outcome.

Here are a few warning signals that your organization may need to reevaluate its processes and mindsets to create a more robust meritocracy for all:

- Does your recruiting or evaluations use the term "culture fit"? That's often code for "looks like me" or "has a shared background, which I favorably advantage."
- Is there verifiable data that shows equal pay in your organization? Statistically, even when women and men work the exact same job, men earn more. Much has been written about this disparity. As Emma Goldberg states in the *New York Times*, "That's partly because women are less likely to negotiate for higher pay and more apt to be penalized when they do."[4] She also quotes C. Nicole Mason, who said, "Instead of being shrewd, a woman negotiating is seen as complaining." What do the statistics in your organization tell you?
- What is the definition of someone being "ready for promotion" versus "not quite ready"? What does the pipeline data show? Is the amount of time it takes to

---

[4] Emma Goldberg, "Knowing What Your Co-Worker Makes Doesn't Close the Pay Gap," *The New York Times*, July 27, 2021, https://www.nytimes.com/2021/07/01/business/salary-transparency-pay-gap.html.

get promoted different for differing groups? McKinsey & Co research indicates that is the case.[5]

- Do you know who is being mentored and who is being sponsored? Mentoring is advising with little at stake, while sponsoring is advocating for another with your own reputation at stake.
- Do you assume everyone is being heard equally? How do you know that?
- Who feels like they belong and are included and who doesn't?
- Do some people have an underlying feeling that diversity means groups that were historically in power are now at a disadvantage? This is often heard by some as "Where are the programs for men?" Maybe there do need to be programs or efforts for all to ensure better leadership, management, and development. But one could argue that actions or programs that help dominant-group men are already in place and include over-sponsorships, uniquely better work assignments, more detailed and focused feedback, greater bonding opportunities with senior leaders, being over-heard or under-scrutinized, under-interrupted, and allowing confidence to cam-

[5] Bryan Hancock and Monne Williams, "One Move Companies Can Take to Improve Diversity," McKinsey, April 9, 2021, https://www.mckinsey.com/featured-insights/diversity-and-inclusion/one-move-companies-can-take-to-improve-diversity.

ouflage lack of competence. These may be acting as subtle programs that have the effect of advancing the men.

- A comment is often made that an organization just can't find enough diverse candidates, which usually means they are fishing from a designated set of ponds, rather than thinking more broadly about where candidates can be found. Or they may decide on a certain criterion for a qualified candidate and then change that criterion when someone they already want to hire comes along.

  As Brogiin Keeton, a senior women lawyer in the financial world who identifies as Black, stated as she talked to me in 2021, "You have to put your money where your mouth is." More than once, she's been asked to help recruit someone diverse to a team. "For a role that fit the credentials and to increase their diversity. I found a Black woman, who did the exact thing they wanted, was in the exact year span, role, all of it. And they say, 'Actually, we feel like somebody a little more senior would be better.' And I'm thinking, 'You should have told me that because I could have found that too.' It's those individual decisions that people make when they think they're in a vacuum that add up."

- Tracking systems for promotions, assignments, feedback, retention, and attrition are lacking or absent.

If your organization has any of these "symptoms," I suggest taking a Meritocracy Stress Test. After the global financial crisis of 2007–2009, bank regulators in the United States and other countries implemented what is known as the bank stress test to ensure that banks had enough capital to withstand an economic or financial crisis. It provides a snapshot into the hypothetical health of a financial institution and its ability to prevent failure, maintain trust, and provide protection to consumers. The annual test outlines categories in a few key areas for evaluation, including level of capital, credit risk, market risk, and liquidity risk. It provides a way for banks to go beyond saying they are financially sound to proving that they truly are.

I propose a similar test for any organization that considers itself a meritocracy. I call it the Meritocracy Stress Test. It is an opportunity for a company to discover whether it is at risk of not being the diverse, inclusive, fair, and equitable workplace it purports to be. To date, every organization I have worked with proclaims it is a meritocracy: the bedrock for values, mission statements, and self-perception. But to prove that shining assertion, there are many questions to ask.

For each of the following propositions, rate your company 1–5, with 1 meaning you haven't focused on this issue, and 5 meaning your organization is completely cognizant of the dynamic and is acting upon it:

1. Engaging in focus groups or surveys with specific members of the company. As mentioned earlier, the framework of the Elephant and the Mouse holds here. We must get better at understanding how everyone in the organization is experiencing the workplace and not assume we have a shared set of experiences. Focus groups, surveys, one-on-one conversations, and listening to employee resource groups are all tools that need to become part of the ongoing lexicon of an organization.

2. Analyzing your data. McKinsey reports that women and other underrepresented groups do get promoted, just at a slower rate than their White male counterparts.[6] Is that true in your company? HR will have the data, so ask them to show you what the speed of promotion looks like for different segments of the company. How many women and people of color are just "not ready" to be promoted? If necessary, hire a data translator who can figure out how to mine the data you have based on the questions that need to be asked.

   Study data on pay gaps and bonus gaps. What does that tell you? Check gender gap reports, such as the World Economic Forum *Global Gender Gap Report*. It can give you a sense of your country rank

---

[6] Sarah Coury, Jess Huang, Ankur Kumar, et al., "Women in the Workplace 2021," McKinsey & Company, September 27, 2021, https://www.mckinsey.com/featured-insights/diversity-and-inclusion/women-in-the-workplace.

and potentially be a reflection of corporate performance overall.

Another area to examine is personnel evaluations: Are women more likely to be criticized for their communication styles than men? One study by Kieran Snyder[7] found that 76% of women's evaluations critiqued them as aggressive and sharp-elbowed, compared to only 2% of men's evaluations.

What does your data show? Even if you have a myriad of programs on DEI, as you assess, don't confuse your efforts around diversity and inclusion with real, measurable outcomes.

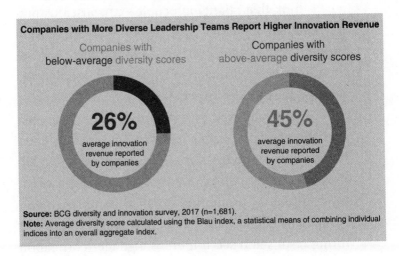

Companies with More Diverse Leadership Teams Report Higher Innovation Revenue

Companies with below-average diversity scores

26% average innovation revenue reported by companies

Companies with above-average diversity scores

45% average innovation revenue reported by companies

Source: BCG diversity and innovation survey, 2017 (n=1,681).
Note: Average diversity score calculated using the Blau index, a statistical means of combining individual indices into an overall aggregate index.

---

[7] Kieran Snyder, "The Abrasiveness Trap: High-Achieving Men and Women Are Described Differently in Reviews," *Fortune*, August 26, 2014, https://fortune.com/2014/08/26/performance-review-gender-bias/.

3. "De-bias" processes at your organization. Whether biases are implicit, unconscious, or conscious, it may be difficult to overcome them, but processes can be de-biased. For example, look at how your company hires and promotes its staff. Check entry job requirements, review past interviews, and consider how you're measuring the culture fit for potential hires. Go back and look at those who were not given a job offer or a promotion. If the issue of culture fit came up, it might mean there is a bias toward those who are like you and perhaps your organization is less diverse as a result.

"I think that changing people's unconscious bias is incredibly difficult," says Keeton. "I believe very strongly in processes, because I think processes are the things that ultimately change people's behaviors because they modify expectations."

Ask yourself whether confidence is being equated to competence. Again, research shows that men believe they are above average, regardless of their abilities, inherently putting them at an advantage when those hiring or promoting conflate confidence and competence. Evaluate job performance reviews or hiring results and see if there is a gender correlation between observed traits of confidence and promotion (or hiring). It is not that women don't think they are above average—about 59% do and to some extent we all have a glorified view of ourselves—but it seems that some funhouse mirrors are more distorted than others.[8]

Herminia Ibarra, the Charles Handy Professor of Organizational Behavior at London Business School, gave a lecture for EDGE in 2021. Professor Ibarra's research indicates that some people get the benefit of the doubt in what they do, while others will elicit cautious concern about their performance. In the Elephant and Mouse world, the Elephant usually gets that assumption of competence and benefit; the Mouse confidence is questioned and seen as more likely to fail. Professor Ibarra sees that women are over-mentored and under-sponsored, given that sponsorship is a more personal, higher-stakes advocacy action. She believes that the more difference there is between two people, the longer it takes to develop a relationship and a comfort with the abilities of the other.

4. Checking your myths and mindsets at the door. As you read the following, reflect on how an organization might believe these statements and what the implications of that might be for different employees:

   • My company is a meritocracy. Only the best rise to the top, getting the promotions and opportunities they deserve.

---

[8] Patrick Heck and Christopher Chabris, "65% of Americans believe they are above average in intelligence: Results of two nationally representative surveys," PLOS ONE, 2018, https://www.ncbi.nlm.nih.gov/pmc/articles/PMC6029792/.

- We have developed and continue to develop programs to help underrepresented groups, including employee resource groups; have specialized training; a designated person for diversity, equity, and inclusion efforts; and highly touted inclusivity statements by senior leaders. Therefore, we must be a fair and meritocratic organization.
- If people only worked harder and asked for what they needed, they would be successful. Everyone gets feedback on their performance and support when they need it.
- Some of the challenges people from underrepresented groups complain about have happened to me in my career, but I overcame them.
- Much more support is being provided to underrepresented groups, and it is now putting White males at a disadvantage.
- Privilege does not exist in a merit-based organization; the playing field is level. Everyone takes an ownership role in making sure that DEI is grounded within everything we do and becomes a touchpoint with as much force as if it were a safety issue.
- Confident people are more competent. The person who always speaks up with their ideas is the person who shows leadership.

THE TEST RESULTS

The numbers that you rated yourself on a 1–5 scale (with 5 being best and 1 meaning a need to review and reflect about the four elements of the Meritocracy Stress Test) can help you tell the story about results, whether people feel included or not. Organizations use data all the time to determine market forces, sales, consumer reactions to products, and quality of their products and services. Data for diversity and inclusion is in its infancy, in comparison. My argument is that the scrutiny and analysis we do within other functions must be used to ensure the outcomes we profess to want for diversity, equity, and inclusion. The leader who commits to DEI will prioritize wanting to know what their data shows.

Wanting to be a meritocracy and actually being one are two different things. The first is an aspiration; the second requires a series of questions and ongoing searching and knowledge and then actions that have impact. Meritocracy is one of those conclusionary words. We describe a firm as meritocratic only if it has all the real workings of a fair organization. The word requires *proof* and not merely the spoken or written promise of it. Declarations are false flags. Take the Meritocracy Stress Test and honestly evaluate your score.

THE ILLUSION OF INCLUSION

Cheryl Kaiser, a professor at the University of Washington, coined the phrase the Illusion of Inclusion (with a strong nod to the work of Patricia Pope, CEO of Pope and Associates). As has been observed previously, her extensive research has shown that the very presence of diversity efforts may give some the illusion that the organization is truly fair, even in the face of evidence that it is not.

Professor Kaiser states, "Implementation of diversity initiatives may ironically work against the (stated) goals of these initiatives by 1) leading people to assume an organization is less discriminatory against minority groups and more discriminatory against majority groups, 2) leading to perceptions of exclusion among members of advantaged groups that can prompt backlash and 3) leading to biased assumptions about the competency of members of disadvantaged groups....One unintended consequence (of diversity efforts) is decreased sensitivity to unfair hiring practices that disadvantage women or minorities....The mere presence of a diversity initiative also makes Whites and men less likely to identify hiring disparities as unfair."[9]

---

[9]Tessa Dover, Cheryl Kaiser, and Branda Major, October 4, 2019, "Mixed Signals: The Unintended Effects of Diversity Initiatives," *Social Issues and Policy Review*, 14(1), pp. 152–181, https://spssi. onlinelibrary.wiley.com/doi/10.1111/sipr.12059.

Frank Dobbin, professor of sociology at Harvard University, has found that young White men feel that a company's announcement and affirmation of diversity training programs is a threat to their own career.[10] The perception is that they will be marginalized and disadvantaged in the face of programs that seek to level the playing field. To them, these programs were a take away, not a remedy.

I remember a fascinating study that asked elementary school teachers to call on boys and girls equally, because there had been reporting that teachers were unknowingly calling on boys more than girls. As best they could, the teachers consciously asked girls and boys equally for responses. After a month or so, the boys were asked what it was like. Their response? The boys felt that girls were getting all of the attention. In their minds, this 50/50 attention was seen as taking something away from them, because they had normalized 60/40 or 70/30 as equal. *Insider Higher Ed* journal reported in June 2021 that males speak 1.6 times more than females in the college classroom.[11] One wonders if the imbalance is noticed or addressed.

---

[10]Frank Dobbin and Alexandra Kalev, "Why Diversity Programs Fail," *Harvard Business Review*, July–August 2016, https://hbr.org/2016/07/why-diversity-programs-fail.

[11]Elizabeth Redden, "Study: Men Speak 1.6 Times More Than Women in College Classrooms," Inside Higher Ed, January 19, 2021, https://www.insidehighered.com/quicktakes/2021/01/19/study-men-speak-16-times-more-women-college-classrooms.

It is crucial that organizations track the impact of diversity efforts and do program evaluations on how these affect hiring, retention, promotion, efforts, perception of inclusion, belonging, and meritocracy. Companies need to message that systems can be made more fair for all and use the technology and other known tools, such as standardized interview techniques, assignment monitoring, and behavior nudges to accomplish that. Continuous engagement among dominant and nondominant groups can reduce archetype beliefs about who others are. Teaching how to be allies, wing persons, and active bystanders can give people a sense they are positively providing change in the workplace without the negative feelings that bias trainings can provoke.

MISTAKE EFFORT FOR OUTCOME

A big mistake in the field of diversity and training is the lack of follow-up to see whether actual change occurs, considering the large amount of an organization's time and expense these efforts consume. The efficacy of diversity initiatives is rarely tracked, Kaiser observes.[12] Companies would never spend millions on marketing products

---

[12] Cheryl Kaiser et al., "Presumed Fair: Ironic Effects of Organizational Diversity Structures." *Journal of Personality and Social Psychology*, 2013, 104 (3): 504–519, https://doi.org/10.1037/a0030838.

or introducing services without looking at the return on their investments. As with leadership training, diversity and inclusion training often does not get the same rigorous attention to outcomes.

Also, by not measuring outcomes, it leaves the organization at risk for actually not knowing what it wants as its objectives. Organizations frequently introduce program after program, such as employee resource groups, donations to minority arts organizations, mentor programs, or high potential initiatives. Each is useful in its own right, but it is an accumulation of efforts that may not align with or abet the overall mission or impact to create a more diverse, inclusive, and meritocratic business. This is reminiscent of an old adage, "If you don't know where you are going, any road will take you there."

Here are some measurable actions to correct for diversity efforts that do not meet the goals sought after. These actions are a way to avoid merely making companies appear responsible or mistakenly believe they are doing the right thing, as shared by Professor Dobbin:

1. Recruit from diverse colleges and professional associations.
2. Offer mentorship to everyone in the organization but also understand the differing consequences of mentoring versus sponsoring.

3. Hire a responsible person or staff to oversee DEI strategies and measure results. Make sure everyone understands their ownership role.

4. Use employee resource groups as one mechanism to hear a collective voice.

5. Train for empathy and opportunities for interaction with different groups, with exercises like writing a few sentences imagining the distinct challenges for someone whose life experiences are substantially different than yours.

6. Create specific metrics (such as year over year numbers that reflect a closing of the meritocracy gap) and then commit to change that can be measured.

7. Validate the efforts of DEI by those in authority and present it as part of the essential strategy and mission of the organization.

8. Reinforce efforts; do not just rely upon one-off programs.

In his book *Thinking, Fast and Slow*, Daniel Kahneman talks about cognitive illusions and how difficult they are to block. "We would all like to have a warning bell that rings loudly whenever we are about to make a serious error, but no such bell is available, and cognitive illusions are generally more difficult to recognize....The voice of reason may be much fainter than the loud and clear voice of an erroneous intuition....The upshot is that it is much easier to identify a minefield when you observe others wandering into it than when you are about to do so."[13]

WHOSE RESPONSIBILITY IS IT? THE SEED AND THE SOIL

Recent discussions about women's careers have focused on the apparent divide between what women should do to ensure their careers go well (Lean In) and what institutions need to do to change policies to help women ensure their careers can be possible, the latter often framed with the question of whether women can have it all. The debate seems to be about which is more important: Does the woman need to be fixed, or is the institution responsible for ensuring policies that support everyone for success?

My response? As professor and author Deborah Tannen once said, that's like asking, "Which line is more important in a rectangle, the long line or the short line?"[14] In a rectangle, both the long and the short lines are

---

[13] Daniel Kahneman, *Thinking, Fast and Slow* (Farrar, Straus and Giroux, 2011).

[14] Deborah Tannen, *Talking from 9 to 5: How Women's and Men's Conversational Styles Affect Who Gets Heard, Who Gets Credit, and What Gets Done at Work* (William Morrow, 1994).

equally essential. So too in careers for women, it is impossible to disaggregate between the individual and the institution. Again, I call this reality the Seed and the Soil: a 50/50 career deal. (I am grateful to my colleague Aynesh Johnson, managing director at Goldman Sachs, who has helped me frame this issue.)

The institution, company, or organization is the Soil. It has a 50% responsibility to make sure supervisors, managers, and leaders develop and maintain awareness that men and women have different approaches (as do other historically underrepresented groups such as Blacks, Asians, the disabled, different cultures, and so on). Most importantly, the institution must give tools to those who lead, and manage these tools to work with those who are different and come from both dominant and nondominant groups. Organizations should not strive for heterogeneity and diversity if the tools and programs are not there to make it work.

On the other hand, who cares most about one's own career? Aside from one's mother, the individual cares most about their career. The individual has a 50% responsibility as the Seed to have the skills, tools, awareness, planning, and personal development to ensure their career goes well.

One example would look like this:

The issue is communication styles. It is known that men and women, and often other cultures, learn through societal example as they grow up to communicate somewhat differently. Not everyone is different, but the cohorts probably speak with slightly different mannerisms.

Women, for example, may use ritual questioning to demand something. Many men realize that when their female partner says, "Do you want to stop for a cup of coffee?" what the woman really means is "Stop now because I want a cup of coffee."

In the workplace, a woman (the Seed) may ask her manager, "Do you think I should get a promotion?" The male manager (the Soil) hears a question and says "No." The Soil has a responsibility to have learned that this is known as a ritual question and to treat it as such. The Seed has a responsibility to realize that there are other speaking frameworks besides ritual question and that she may need to use a different approach, given her intended audience.

This is but a small example of a situation that abounds in the workplace. Yes, women should lean into their careers and understand how to stay engaged if they off-ramp for a time, speak up, ask for their assignments, get critical feedback, seek promotions, state their accomplishments, and learn more ways to behave other than just those understood through societal norms. It is 50% their responsibility to stretch themselves and get out of their comfort zones.

But there is a similar 50% responsibility from the institution, as represented by the managers, supervisors, and leaders, to be taught and to understand the implications of their requirements for long hours of face time, for the unconscious negative career consequences of doing telework, flex work, or hitting the career pause button. They must understand exactly how a double bind works and how they may be engaging in one (assertive men versus aggressive women), and to learn what disarming mechanisms are, including ritual apology, question, mitigation, modesty, humility, and smiling.

The institution has to make managers far more aware of how "like" gravitates to "like," how people bond with those who are similar to them, and to mitigate the consequences of this in hierarchical organizations where rewards are given out unequally. The organization, if it is going to state that its goal is to have a diverse workforce for its innovation and creativity, then must teach managers to appreciate that some people have no trouble stating how good and accomplished they are, and some people have a background that taught them not to brag.

Organizations teach their employees how to handle diverse technical products and diverse ways to generate revenue. They know that nourishing excellence in employees requires a fertile soil. Organizations provide constant attention, metrics, training, examples, behavior modifications, penalties, rewards, and recognition when it comes to issues like safety or product purity. Having an organization filled with diverse individuals also requires that same level of rich soil.

The individual will only flower if there is a strong seed, which they must come to provide to the organization to make their own careers blossom.

THE SEED AND THE SOIL: IT TAKES BOTH

We all need ways to monitor ourselves relying upon our illusions, myths, and fables about who others are. We need humans and nonhumans to help us to discern between what we think is real and what is truly reality. The first step in overcoming the blind spots of our illusions, myths, mindsets, and unfounded beliefs is to realize they all exist.

This is about decades of conditioning. Decades in our lifetime, but centuries in the scope of our country and our society that predisposes you to make certain assessments and to make them extremely rapidly.

I've conceived of a model that I call the Bond assessment, as in James Bond with his quick reflexes, inspired by research that suggested that in 7/1000 of a second, we critique a stranger on their physical attributes. In another four-tenths of a second, we formulate an action plan on how to deal with a stranger. Now, most of us don't feel intense in thousands of a second. That is half a heartbeat. Not knowing this, people really believe they just need to have a positive attitude. No, you need to understand what you're up against, and then hold yourself accountable for those decisions.

Assumptions lead to conclusions. Conclusions lead to decisions. And decisions have consequences.

Chapter 5

What You Can Do Easily

The rest of the sentence in the chapter title is "I may not be able to do at all." A parent tells their child, "Be creative." A police officer shouts, "Calm down." A boss gives feedback, "Say what you think." These are all potential no-win situations. How does one force someone to be creative on demand? If a police officer is shouting at someone to calm down, the circumstances are probably quite fraught with anxiety. The manager who tells you to say what you think may not realize that you will be judged in a particular way depending upon your gender or other status.

IT IS NOT THE NORM

These are all called double binds, and they occur more frequently in the workplace than may be realized. Once someone is in a double bind, it is almost impossible to get it right. This can be a heavy weight on those who find themselves caught in the narrow canyon of behavior that a double bind forces upon them.

Merriam-Webster's dictionary describes a "double bind" as "a psychological predicament in which a person receives from a single source conflicting messages that allow no appropriate response to be made," and lists synonyms as "catch-22," "dilemma," and "quandary."

The literature on women and diversity has often referenced this double bind. Kathleen Hall Jamieson, the director of the Annenberg Public Policy Center, wrote a book about the subject.[1] For example, it often means women have a narrow band of behavior that is socially acceptable. If they go beyond that band they can be criticized. It is the proverbial "damned if you do and damned if you don't."

Another example is when a politician responds to a rumor or negative story, it provides more oxygen to the rumors or possible falsities. If the person does not respond, people assume they must be guilty of what the rumor is alleging. Former U.S. Senator Barbara Mikulski used to quip that if a high-level woman leader is single, she must not be able to get a man. If the woman is married, she must be neglecting the man. If she is divorced, she obviously drove him away, and if she is widowed, she killed him.

---

[1] Kathleen Hall Jamieson, *Beyond the Double Bind: Women and Leadership* (Oxford University Press, 1995).

In today's world this double bind is cause for concern and presents a roadblock toward achieving the goals of diversity, equity, and inclusion. This bind can be a definite drag on women and other groups' ability to function freely and well in an organization. It is a drain and a distraction for the people who have to be so hypervigilant, and it is an indication that the organization does not have a good grasp about how people experience the workplace.

Let's look at further examples. A White man gets feedback he doesn't like. He has the luxury of getting upset, even showing some anger because he is socially able to get away with that without punishment. White women, Black women, and Black men usually don't have that flexibility to show their true emotions. Generally, LGBTQ, people of color, or those from differing nationalities must tread with caution. They are haunted by the possibility of being negatively labeled with attributes such as brazen, aggressive, hysterical, hypersensitive, unable to manage their emotions, or unable to take criticism. Black people have an even narrower band in which to operate before they fall victim to the perception of "angry Black man" or "angry Black woman" or being viewed as potentially dangerous, uppity, pushy, or acting above their social station.

President Obama was often seen as cool, not prone to anger. That may or may not have been the feelings he felt inside. He could have been seething with anger but knew better than to show those emotions. How exhausting.

A colleague, a Black man, told me about a time he was gesturing to make a point in a meeting. He was, he said, tapping his finger on the table to reinforce the comment. Another colleague came up to him afterwards and asked why he was "banging" on the table. My friend was astonished at how he was perceived.

What is the other part of the bind in that feedback example? For the woman, she gets critical feedback and feels the desire to cry, probably out of frustration and disappointment. Well, she can't do that either because of the stigma of being considered not tough enough. If she just "manned up," she would be seen as handling it well. And yet if she did, she would be perceived as unseemly and unlikeable.

Of course, men of any group can't really cry. It is almost universally unacceptable (although we can hope this is changing). So, men, particularly White men, have one bind but they don't have two, which is what leaves people no room to maneuver in the double bind. It is well known that when women behave in a dominant or assertive style, they are not well liked. If they behave in a less assertive style they are not seen as leaders. Their choice is nice versus competent. Often, White men can be both assertive and well liked or assertive and not well liked and this has little effect on their success.

This goes much further with some dominant-group men. The rage, anger, and wildly inappropriate aggression (yelling, throwing things) in professional situations

I've seen is astonishing. Generally, that wide bandwidth of behavior directly correlates with levels of power or control over others. Behavior from these individuals—whatever it is (and I'm putting aside sexual aggression and sexual assault)—is largely shrugged off. This dominant group of men can act however they want. ("Oh, he's just like that," or "Oh, that's his thing," or "Boys will be boys.") The consequences for them may be minimal to none. If a woman, or other nondominant group member, screams and shouts at their employees in an office, they may be labeled difficult, not leader-like, or too emotional.

Gay men have often learned to use humor, a skill developed at an early age, to deflect bullies from attacking them. But use of humor too often in the workplace may make them seem less serious. However, acting without humor can mean the loss of a potential defense mechanism in the face of potential homophobia. Asian men and women can fall into perceptions that they may not be recognized as leaders, as they may behave in a more relational or shared community manner rather than in a more individualistic way. However, if they do take on a transactional, individualistic manners, they may be perceived as betraying cultural norms.

Women and other minority groups are constantly walking a tightrope that is invisible to the dominant group. The Elephant may not be aware of the differing standards that are being placed on the Mouse and the possibility of negative reactions to behaviors that the

Elephant would never receive. The Elephant really hasn't a clue that this calculus is a constant for the Mouse. This can have a knock-on effect if a dominant group mentor coaches someone who may be more subject to double binds, to just do something the Mouse knows will not work for them. "Just speak up, just demand the promotion, just state how good you are" may not be as useful as more nuanced approaches might be. But the Elephant needs to understand why the nuance is necessary.

Another example of what is acceptable for some and not for others includes talking about "I" versus playing up the team. To play the "I" game can be tricky for some. Women in particular are often held to the archetype of the ones who should take care of others. Their individual needs or voices can take others by surprise. Hopefully this is changing as more women take on leadership roles, entrepreneurial efforts, or political positions. However, even if the roles taken are impressively accomplished, there is often still a need to minimize their own personal ambitions for the benefit of the group. "I versus we" is still a tightrope they must walk.

A small test: when you listen to someone, count how many "I" statements they use and what you think is acceptable as part of a natural and positive sense of self. How many times can a man say "I" and how many times can a woman say "I" before, in your own mind, each tips over into unacceptable self-aggrandizing behavior?

Here is an interesting distinction: In some countries with great wealth disparity between the rich and the poor, the rich person, whether a woman or a man, can be much more "I" focused than a poor person working for that rich person. It is often ultimately about dominance and nondominance.

Speaking frequently versus not speaking enough is another indication of the difference between groups. In her blog "Language in the Wild," Valerie Fridland, PhD, explores the mistaken notion that women talk too much. She reflects back to Greek and Roman times when the notion was that only men were to speak in the public sphere and women had no place there.[2] When women did speak, their talk was trivialized or seen as irritating (think of Shakespeare's *Taming of the Shrew*). As Dr. Fridland reports, "It would appear that we still hold dearly to the idea that women remain the great trivializers of talk, and that speech in the public domain is best left to men. For instance, well-known research by education scholars Myra and David Sadker and Nancy Zittleman found that boys take up the majority of class talking time. Similarly, women have been found to contribute less in professional settings, where men tend to control the conversational floor."

---

[2] Valerie Fridland, "Language in the Wild," *Psychology Today*, 2020.

Yet ask most people which is the most talkative sex, and they will doubtless offer up women. Teachers in those same studies that found more talking time for boys, reported feeling that girls took up more of their time in class. In reality, they actually gave more attention to boys by calling on them frequently while they interrupted girls' talk more. Early then begins the long process of disempowering girls by treating their talk as marginal and unwelcome.

This suggests that our long-held beliefs about women's speech create subtle but very real obstacles to women's contribution to and success in professional, institutional, and educational arenas. Linguist Deborah Tannen, who has studied gender and workplace language, suggests that women are more reticent to talk or self-promote when in contexts typically dominated by men.

This, of course, may impact their competitiveness for promotions and leadership positions by those higher up, though it is not clear that women speaking up would be received well. Research by psychologist Victoria Brescoll looking at the distribution of talk by gender shows that institutional power encourages men but discourages women from talking more, as powerful women fear a backlash that is absent for men when taking on a greater share of the conversational floor.[3]

---

[3] Ibid.

Thus, the double bind for women is if you speak up, you may be irritating and taking up more than your entitled space. But if you don't speak up, you confirm that you have nothing to contribute to the important issues of the day. We can also imagine the same goes for other groups who have not historically been welcome in the public space and whose ideas have not been considered valuable to be heard.

ASKING FOR A PROMOTION VERSUS LOOKING AGGRESSIVE

Promoting yourself versus promoting others, stating credentials versus appearing to brag, stating accomplishments versus being humble, having career goals versus being seen as overly ambitious, portraying yourself as self-assured versus seeming overconfident: these are all style dilemmas. Everyone can fall into the negative side of the equation, but the key here is how much can you convey *before* you are considered cocky, a braggart, or overly aggressive. For dominant groups, the leeway is wider; for nondominant groups, particularly if you act outside accepted norms, the bandwidth is much narrower.

The litmus test is always simple. If the behavior, or the frequency of the behavior, is acceptable to members of the dominant group, it must be acceptable for nondominant groups' members to do the *exact* same thing.

Confidence versus competence means how good I think I am versus how good others think I am. Let me quote a story from Tomas Chamorro-Premuzic's book *Why Do So Many Incompetent Men Become Leaders?* He describes two colleagues, Shilpa and Ryan, at a large global accounting firm: "Although Shilpa is more qualified and experienced than Ryan, they are paid the same. Shilpa has been with the firm for five more years than Ryan has, but Ryan made such an impression during his job interview that he was hired at Shilpa's level despite being less qualified. His self-regard is apparent not only during job interviews, but also in internal team assignments, client presentations, and networking events."

Ryan speaks more, and louder than Shilpa does, and is much more likely to interrupt others in his enthusiasm to share ideas, which he loves to present. He's less likely to qualify his statements with caveats and more likely to speak in bold strokes—something his boss sees as "having vision." When he and Shilpa present recommendations to clients, Ryan does most of the talking. When clients ask questions, Shilpa is likely to provide a range of options. If she is stumped, she'll admit it. But Ryan never hedges. He usually comes up with a single recommended course of action. And if a client asks him something he doesn't know, he'll skillfully dodge the question. Accordingly, their boss assumes Shilpa is less confident, and consequently less competent. Eventually, Ryan is promoted to a leadership role, while Shilpa remains where she is.[4]

The relationship between confidence and competence may be tenuous at best, if it exists at all. And yet we consistently urge women to be more confident. I hear less discussion about asking male leaders to be more competent. These guardrails for women and other underrepresented groups mean they are far more limited in the range of human behaviors and emotions they are able to employ to express their needs, desires, and goals. It means they must exhaust their energy censoring themselves or finding that narrow passage to navigate to be seen as normal, not offensive, and acceptable to those who are judging them.

Imagine what it would be like if you were only allowed to use certain words, express certain attitudes, self-censor, or be ever vigilant for what might offend. The burden and effort of that is enormous, exhausting, and certainly not fair. If you cherish and seek diversity, equity, and inclusion, those goals take a real hit because of the dynamics related here.

---

[4] Tomas Chamorro-Premuzic, *Why Do So Many Incompetent Men Become Leaders? (And How to Fix It)* (Harvard Business Review Press, 2019).

What can help alleviate that burden? Here is one exercise: Try a reverse role play. Imagine that someone who is not like you—because of race, gender, identity, nationality—is acting in a way that bothers you because they are behaving in a manner that seems out of character with how you expect them to act.

Let's say a woman is firmly stating her beliefs in a meeting and acting in a way you think is too assertive. Play a game with yourself. Think of how you would react if a man were doing the exact same thing; let's say your friend John. Would you think he was talking appropriately, or would you consider his actions too assertive? If the latter, then maybe your assessment is correct. If the former, you are laboring under a false belief about what is correct behavior and making a judgment that will cloud how you perceive that woman. She is not making you uncomfortable; she is acting normally using a full range of emotions. You are making *yourself* uncomfortable, but blaming her.

Ask a woman or other nondominant colleague what they concern themselves with in the workplace and check to see if these are similar to your own concerns. When a woman or other nondominant person walks into a meeting, they are thinking about how they're dressed, where to sit, how exactly to speak, what people are assuming, how to handle a subtle or less than subtle put-down, how to respond to questions about their competency, how to demonstrate confidence without being perceived as overbearing, or how they might be tested and not even know the criteria by which they are being judged. They may struggle to bond with colleagues before the meeting who are talking about a subject the nondominant person has little interest in or knowledge of.

The Elephant, or dominant person, may be thinking about his preparation, whom he can bond or banter with, what will satisfy the boss, or what chair he will strategically sit in—but not any of the other concerns related above. Within the schema of the Elephant and the Mouse, we know the Mouse has to multitask. It has to listen acutely to hear when the Elephant is showing up. It needs to sense the mood of the other larger entity to figure out how to placate it, work around it, distract it, humor it, and maneuver artfully.

Some men, at times, become uncomfortable when they find themselves the only man in the room. All of a sudden, they don't quite know how to act, what the rules of the road are, how to say things without potential for misinterpretation. They have not had to spend years honing their skill sets of observation and readjusting behavior toward the other. It has not been necessary for their own survival or success to have a constant awareness and concern about someone who is not like them.

In *The Loudest Duck*, I suggested keeping an ear out for the use of the words "too" or "not enough." She's too aggressive; he is not strong enough. Any combination of those kinds of conclusions is usually a tip-off that you are walking in the world differently and have foregone beliefs about how others should properly behave.

Check your data to see if this imbalance is happening, for example, in the review and evaluation processes. The previously mentioned study by Kieran Snyder highlighting gender discrepancies in the tech industry showed that negative personal criticism appeared in 2.4% of reviews of men and 76% of women's.[5] As Mark Kaplan of Dagoba Group referenced in my 2021 interview with him, "Look for patterns. What assumptions are here, and what questions need to be asked? There is a need to bring people's attention to patterns and where these dynamics are real.... Don't expect Human Resources to do this for you."

My suggestion is that organizations need to create "The Easy to Do Test." Survey employees across a selection of actions, such as promoting oneself, speaking in meetings, or asking for a raise. Separate the data by various diverse groups and see what the results are. If there are gaps in what different groups consider easy or not easy to do, you then have a roadmap for intervention and for creating tools and systems to ensure that what is easy for some to do becomes easy for all to do.

Be curious. Ask someone who is different than you about their strategy for speaking, asking for something,

---

[5] Kieran Snyder, "The Abrasiveness Trap: High-Achieving Men and Women Are Described Differently In Reviews," *Fortune*, August 26, 2014, https://fortune.com/2014/08/26/performance-review-gender-bias/.

presenting themselves in meetings or Zoom calls, and getting or giving feedback. Make note of how much or how little they contend with as they maneuver through their day or even through their career. It may give you a window into a world you never even knew existed.

It is a simple given to say that we all live in different worlds. It is important to note, though, that while our individual experiences are unique, there are elements of similarity depending upon the group we belong to, particularly when it comes to contrasting (and potentially judging) the lived expressions of differing groups.

Some find it easy to say and do certain things; they are accepted, reinforced, and judged positively. But as this chapter suggests, there are those who don't reflect the norms of the dominant group or don't belong to it but spend much of their life mixing with that group. Their careers and livelihoods may depend upon the understanding that diversity creates full belonging and inclusion only with the conscious awareness that what's easy for you to say or do may not be easy for others.

Chapter 6

We Are All Human, with Help from Nonhumans

If we assume that humans are an amalgam of characteristics, some useful and some not so useful, then we all need help, particularly in a world that is diverse and seeks to have everyone feel included while sharing a sense of communal equity. The basic assumption is that we have unconscious and conscious beliefs about who other people are and we react based on those beliefs, assumptions, and archetypes. Much controversy exists around whether we can truly eliminate bias from our internal psyches.

In their seminal *Harvard Business Review* article, Frank Dobbin and Alexandra Kalev argue that it is futile to continue the exercise of unconscious bias training and that these trainings can actually make situations worse.[1] Some White people end up feeling that the very presence of diversity efforts means that they are being treated unfairly. Anti-bias training can embed stereotypes rather than eliminate them. People who go through these trainings feel they have license not to embrace diversity by

[1] Frank Dobbin and Alexandra Kalev, "Why Diversity Programs Fail," *Harvard Business Review*, July–August 2016, https://hbr.org/2016/07/why-diversity-programs-fail.

the very fact they have gone through the training. (Think: I can eat French fries because I drank a diet soft drink.)

As Brogiin Keeton points out, "If you are leveling the playing field, then you are taking away an unfair advantage. It doesn't necessarily mean you're adding a headwind to cis White males, if I'm going to pick on that population, but it does mean you're taking away some of their tailwind. And I think that we have to kind of be honest about that, and from a structural perspective understand that people are going to be annoyed when they experience that. I think if you've never experienced that before, it's really annoying. We have to prepare people for that and prepare them for what real equality looks like."

I share the trepidation that comes with unconscious bias trainings and the side effects those trainings expose. My belief is that there are four ways (and probably more) to change behavior:

1. Change individual behaviors.
2. Change systems and structures.
3. Provide a lifeline through intervention by others.
4. Add nonhuman ways to analyze, nudge, aid, and correct behavior.

This chapter looks at how other humans and nonhumans can both help an individual's behaviors and shape the systems and structures within an organization.

When I was young, I loved the *Wizard of Oz*. Little did I know at that young age that each character represented figures in the debate over gold versus silver, that the ruby red slippers of technicolor were originally silver, or that Frank Baum, the 1890s author, despised Native Americans. All I saw was the fable and the three figures that represented brains (the Scarecrow), heart (the Tin man), and courage (the Lion). They joined up to help Dorothy find her way home when she confronted dangers on the Yellow Brick Road. They helped her deal with the poppy field (now I understand why Dorothy got sleepy!), the flying monkeys, and the wicked witches. Dorothy needed support to get to her destination. We all need human support to help us navigate our world. In my view, it shows itself at minimum in three forms: the wingman or wing woman, the ally, and the independent interlocutor/scribe (and the interlocuter's cousin, the active bystander).

THE WINGMAN OR WING WOMAN

The concept of the wingman originated in the military and is nearly as old as fighter aviation. The wingman's role is to support others in aerial combat to help make flying safer by amplifying awareness of what's happening around them that might not be in the sights of the first pilot. The wingman or wing woman pilots a plane that flies just outside and behind the right wing of the leading aircraft in a flight formation, in order to provide protective support. (Of course, nowadays a wingman or wing woman has also come to refer to someone who helps you get a date at a bar!)

In the workplace, everyone needs this extra pair of eyes and ears. They are your own personal defender, usually a friend or close colleague who stands up for you when they see habits or wrongs that need righting. During the Obama presidential years, the senior women in the administration pledged to step in and support their female colleagues when they observed them not being taken seriously or when their ideas and voices needed amplifying. As Vox news reporter Emily Crockett wrote, quoting a report by Juliet Eilperin in the *Washington Post*:

> When President Obama took office, two-thirds of his top aides were men. Women complained of having to elbow their way into important meetings. And when they got in, their voices were sometimes ignored.

> So female staffers adopted a meeting strategy they called "amplification": When a woman made a key point, other women would repeat it, giving credit to its author. This forced the men in the room to recognize

the contribution—and denied them the chance to claim the idea as their own.[2]

Crockett continues, "For most women in the workplace, this phenomenon is exhaustingly familiar: A woman offers an idea in a meeting, but nobody notices or acknowledges it until a man later says the same thing."
Are women imagining this? No:

Decades of research show that women get interrupted more often—by both men and women—and that women are given less credit, or even penalized, for speaking out more.

The solution Obama's female staffers came up with is genius. It's a great model for women everywhere who are frustrated with the status quo of *manterruption* and *bropropriation*, and other silly new words for all the serious old things women have always dealt with but never named.

It shows that when women band together and support one another, it can be incredibly powerful....

---

[2] Emily Crockett, "The Amazing Tool That Women in the White House Used to Fight Gender Bias," Vox, September 14, 2016, https://www.vox.com/2016/9/14/12914370/white-house-obama-women-gender-bias-amplification.

But it also shows just how much conscious effort is required to overcome biases against women, especially women in power.[3]

The wing person watches out to ensure their protectee is not interrupted, by using simple techniques such as "Hold on Andrew, I'd like to hear Mary finish." They can notice that an expert on a topic who is hearing impaired and needs a sign interpreter knows much more than the person speaking as if they were the expert. The wing person makes known to the group that a particular colleague is the true expert and invites them to take the stage to communicate. The supporter can go to bat for another by stating the accomplishment of the more humble employee and championing their advancement. Diversity, equity, and inclusion are only abstract concepts unless they are practiced in the real-life manifestations of everyday inequity.

I'm particularly fond of having cross-diversity wing people. Thus, a White person champions a Hispanic/Latino person, or a woman steps in for a shy man on the team. The shock of what might seem out of character can often have a more dramatic impact than same/same reinforcement. In a subtle or not so subtle way, the wing person is also pointing out the unnerving habits of others and flagging dynamics that are occurring in the moment. These

---

[3] Ibid.

become "teachable" moments. Negative micro-actions can unlevel the diverse playing field and small positive micro-actions can rebalance those scales to level the field.

THE ALLY

Much has been written of late about the role of the ally in the realm of human support needed to create a fairer world, particularly when it comes to social, racial, and other justice issues. Often there is a misconception that this is some King Arthur figure who can swoop in, pull the sword out of the stone, and be the savior of the downcast. The misguided sense is that it is about noblesse oblige, coming to the rescue of the downtrodden, but in reality the ally must work hard to become a true and meaningful actor to advance equality. Unlike the wingman who reacts always in the moment, the ally has a longer arch of connection and wider aperture.

We have seen programs developed by the United Nations like "HE for SHE," which enlists celebrities, world leaders, global CEOs, and academic heads who share their tried and tested best practices to solve some of today's biggest gender issues like gender bias, violence against women, and equality. Australia's Sex Discrimination Commissioner Elizabeth Broderick created Champions of Change, getting male CEOs of the biggest companies in Australia to make commitments in support of promoting and developing women in their firms. It became so popular that male leaders felt they must join and commit to be considered strong advocates.

Ultimately allies have a common interest in ensuring the ones they align with become part of a fairer system. They do leverage their own position of power (some call it privilege) to educate others, provide support, and amplify voices more broadly. This person has significant "assets" they can spend on behalf of others. Unlike a charitable donation, though, the assets do not diminish, but rather can increase with the growth of the wisdom gained by being an ally. They don't speak on behalf of those who are facing issues that keep them from fully flourishing; they speak to others in their own group, pointing the way to make their environment a better place.

To be an ally is not for the faint at heart. At times an ally is standing up against the norm, against the commonly held beliefs, or against their own peers.

Steven Frost, CEO of D&I consultancy Included, shares this: "Like other diversity and inclusion initiatives, allyship can be viewed with a little trepidation, and considered something that has to be learned and used in a certain way. However at its most simple, allyship is about helping others to feel confident in themselves, to feel supported, to feel included, and therefore able to maximize their potential."[4]

---

[4] Deirdre Golden, "Walking in Allyship," Included, May 6, 2021, https://www.included.com/walking-in-allyship/.

An ally seeks to understand the life experience of someone from a different background or group, including them, and speaking up for them.

Effective allyship is about listening to the individual, seeking to understand them, taking direction from them, asking questions about their life experience, and speaking up for them....

Employee networks are increasingly keen to promote allyship. We are hearing more about male allies, partly as a response to the #MeToo movement, but also as a way for men to show their active support for women in the workplace. With the catalyst of the #BlackLivesMatter movement and increasing awareness of intersectional experiences, we have an important opportunity to expand this further.

Finally, effective allyship is active allyship, and organizations should consider providing guidelines on how to be an active ally, standing up for under-represented groups, and promoting inclusion and belonging.[5]

Allyship can be taught. It is about noticing, and as Stephen Frost mentions, guidelines can be provided, and

---

[5] Ibid.

actions observed. Consider these tips for practicing to be an ally:

- Listen to those whose life experiences differ from yours and make no internal mental edits or disclaimers to what they express as their lived world. A senior male executive of Hispanic descent from a financial services company shared that early in his career he felt compelled to fit in and "unlearn" some of the habits and expressions he used growing up. He had to comply with a style of speaking that was in some ways like talking in a foreign language. He knew that his bosses had no idea the effort it took for him and always wished someone would have asked him about his lived experiences.

- Ask what support is actually needed, not what support you think is needed. I once had a boss who felt like he was helping me in meetings. He would add on after I had spoken and explain, "What Laura is trying to say is…" This was embarrassing and certainly was not helping develop my credibility, nor was it improving my ability to express myself clearly.

- Share with your own group what you are learning and help others to learn what you are learning. Simple questions such as "Are you married?" or "Planning to have kids?" might feel inoffensive and friendly to some, while having differing consequences when said to a woman, or to an LGBTQ person who is not yet ready to come out.

- The reward of allyship is contained in the act of doing. Acknowledgment and praise are nice but not necessarily what will be evidenced from those you ally with.

THE INDEPENDENT INTERLOCUTOR/SCRIBE

This new role is only now starting to be seen as valuable. This is a person, unconnected to any of the parties in a particular situation, who can play the part of the "grand inquisitor." They are independent eyes and ears to point out dynamics that may be playing out unbeknownst to those in the midst of the action.

I have seen these people be particularly effective in personnel evaluations, promotion decisions, meeting or classroom dynamics, situations of under- or over-hearing, and assignments. This person need not be from the outside of the organization, but should have the ability to speak up and to challenge powerful people who need to be guided. Usually, it is someone outside the reporting structure, so they don't feel in anyway pressured. Outside consultants can also be brought in. Outsiders should have knowledge of the industry because they will need to be seen as credible to the understanding of a particular workplace.

This independent arbiter can be someone from inside but, generally speaking, an outsider has more bandwidth and credibility to intervene and point out what they are seeing.

They should be well versed in the subtle inequities that can happen that go unnoticed in the normal course of our interactions.

An example of how that might work was demonstrated at the Harvard Business School. (I am an alum of HBS.) Starting in 2013, HBS uncovered that women were not succeeding as the school expected they would. The discovery came through data that showed that women were not becoming Baker Scholars, an accomplishment awarded to the top 5% of the class and recognition of graduation with distinction. This is a highly prized award when students are being recruited for jobs. Women were over 35% of the students, yet less than 13% of the Baker Scholars. Because of this, the school took a number of steps, including the placement of scribes in the classroom. They tracked who talked by gender, how long the men and women talked (yes, men talked on average longer than women), who raised their hands to be called upon, and what comments the professors wrote on the board. They noted whether the professors referred to one gender more often (to the men more than the women) and observed whether attribution of comments was given to the right person. This information was then shared with the professors to give them a mirror into their classroom actions and to correct for unconscious and possibly biased memories of who said what. Given how important classroom participation was in the evaluation of students, these dynamics were freighted with disproportionate importance.

Both men and women professors found themselves overemphasizing the men in the room and were surprised to learn they were doing so. HBS also looked at the culture of the classroom, noting that argumentative styles and negotiating were prized approaches to dealing with the cases. Collaborating and collective agreement were not. Aggressive hand raising was the norm. They also noted that men went to the professors more frequently during office hours than did women. All of this contributed to a sense of inequality and preference for dominant-group behavior. Once these issues were unveiled, the school was able to even out the dynamics so that the professors were conscious of what they were doing and could change behavior. Now the women are represented slightly more as Baker Scholars than their actual school representation in the class.

Corporations that do performance reviews can use this concept as a way to listen to the discussions and evaluate individuals to see if the same behaviors in men are being cast in different light compared to the behaviors of women and minorities. A manager may reflect on a man's performance, noting he speaks his mind, is not afraid to confront conflict, and shows assertive confidence in his speaking style, and conclude he is therefore a good candidate for a promotion. The same manager evaluates the woman on his team and remarks that she is often too aggressive, stating her positions forcefully, bragging about her credentials and successes, and is too willing to confront others. He concludes she is not yet ready for a promotion and needs time to develop further communication skills. The independent listener raises the question of why two people who are seemingly doing the same thing are characterized so differently.

This independent person can also sit in on meetings periodically and track the dynamics of the group interaction. That tracking might include who does and does not speak, how long people speak for, who interrupts whom, whether there is a perception that ideas are being repeated and acknowledged not because of who said it first but because of whom the speaker is. A report back to the manager of the meeting could contain surprising and valuable insight into whether she or he is truly creating a fully inclusive exchange of ideas.

ACTIVE BYSTANDER

The independent interventionist has a cousin who can be labeled the active bystander, or the new term Upstander. This is a role any one of us can play and the idea of this is to step in when we see a problematic situation. We would expect that anyone would feel compelled to step in if there was a safety issue in the workplace.

In the police force this person is usually another police officer, and has a responsibility, some would say duty, to stop a potentially harmful situation from getting to a danger point for an officer or citizen.

This role requires each of us to see ourselves as an agent of action, permitted to take responsibility, even morally obligated to do so. It can have a profound effect on stopping actions that could be deemed unduly threatening to a particular group or person, often someone of a different race, gender, sexual identity, or nationality.

We each have more power than we realize and can both influence and be a role model for others. Simple gestures can have long-lasting impact. A colleague told me a story about her boss. She was his executive assistant, and he was the CEO of the organization. His office sat at the end of a hallway, so no one could actually just "wander by" when going from one part of the building to another. She noticed with slight amazement and humor that some men just happened to wander by his office, stop in for a chat, and wander back away. She never saw a woman or a person of color do so. After several months, she told the CEO of her observations. He had never noticed it. Fortunately for him, he realized the subtle impact of these casual drive-bys that allowed him to get to informally know some but not others. He personally devised a scheduled meetup with a wider range of individuals. Without the observation and intervention by his executive assistant, it is possible that this uneven access could have continued.

When I was a police officer, my assigned partner and I would watch for signs that the other was getting tunnel vision, overly reactive, or emotionally fraught. It never escalated to the threat of bodily harm, but we needed to step in at times and say, "I'll take care of this now," or "Let me handle this one." One of the officers I worked with was quick to stop someone from showing disrespect to either him or me. He stepped in rapidly to deflect that. I would usually let the person show disrespect once before I engaged, but not allow it a second time. Sometimes my partner was right; it was dangerous to let the other person think they got the upper hand from the start. Sometimes I was right to keep the escalation from occurring and putting all parties into a dangerous jam.

Every organization needs wing persons, allies, independent interlocutors, and active bystanders. Institutions need people who observe and step in as best they can. (We also need mentors and sponsors, and I think most organizations have already got those on their radar.) Power is meted out unevenly in any organization; some individuals have quite a bit and others are at the mercy of the more powerful. And we are all human. Like Dorothy, we depend upon each other in the DEI space to help get to where we say we want to go.

NONHUMAN HELP

Why do we need nonhuman help in our decision-making? Our brains are not machines. We are an amalgam of many inputs when we make decisions or filter information.

As mentioned, these frameworks come from Grandma and they include anecdotes, learned history, tribal knowledge, instinct, and gut feelings. Talk to any family therapist, who will tell you that each child raised in a family has a different set of stories about what their family was like. In some cases, differing mirrors into the world are harmless. But diversity puts a price tag on the baggage we bring into our workspace.

So we do need nonhuman help. I am referring to tools we can engage that substitute for our own archetypical unconscious thinking. These are tools that can help us realize that intuition or assumed knowledge are not as reliable as we think they are. Tools are aids to show us where there are patterns of actions and decisions we might not see and impacts we may not realize.

In her book, *What Works: Gender Equality by Design*, Iris Bohnet observes, "When it comes to improving our people decisions, few new tools promise to revolutionize human resource management as thoroughly as people analytics....In its simplest form, people analytics collects large amounts of data and uses complex applications to measure relationships between variables and detect patterns and trends."[6] As data analytics increases in usage, it is also important to be mindful of what data is being collected and for what purpose. Some raise the cautionary

---

[6] Iris Bohnet, *What Works: Gender Equality by Design* (Belknap Press, 2016).

note that artificial intelligence (AI) is only as good as the (possibly biased) assumptions built into the artificial thinking.

What are some uses of people analytics that might be appealing? Google is at the forefront of this use. They have figured out by analyzing the data that what looked like a gender gap in retention was actually a "parent gap." They changed their maternity and paternity leave plan and removed the gap entirely.

As Dean Bohnet observed, Google also used data to figure out the best predictors of an employee's likelihood of leaving and therefore what were the needed interventions. She presents another example, of a financial institution that kept paying women less on their sales because it seemed that they sold less. The immediate assumption was that the women were not as good as the men, confirming what some believed was the "reduction of meritocracy" by putting women in these positions.

A deeper dive into the data suggested something entirely different was actually causing the discrepancy.[7] It turned out that the women were being treated differently and were being assigned inferior accounts and sales opportunities.

As I mentioned before, I once worked with an organization that assigned research to individual associates and analysts. With a closer look at the data, we found that the

---

[7] Ibid.

men were getting the large-capital manufacturing companies for their research assignments. The women were assigned the small- to medium-capital service companies, with the consequence that women were not achieving the visibility and rewards the men were. The good news is that, generally speaking, once companies see the data anomalies, they have the wherewithal to fix the discrepancies and even out the playing field.

Mercer and RedThread Research created a compendium of 105 companies working in the D&I technology space. I do not endorse any of the companies they highlight, but it is a robust sweep of what is possible in the people analytics field now. Two examples are companies called Textio and Humanyze. Again, no endorsement here, but a show of what is possible. I quoted Kieran Snyder of Textio previously about the differential in performance reviews of women and those of men, with women getting far more criticisms of their communication styles, along with more personality-based feedback than men. Women's reviews were five times more critical than men's, and while men's feedback was results oriented, women's was more personality oriented.[8]

Kieran founded Textio and created software that she describes as bias interrupters. Her company discovered

---

[8] "The Rise of a Transformative Market," Mercer, 2019, https://www.mercer.com/our-thinking/career/diversity-and-inclusion-technology.html.

that certain words in job descriptions were more likely to attract people based on race or gender. For example, underrepresented groups did not like jargon words such as "synergy" or "leveraging." Women were less attracted to descriptions of jobs that were seen as competitive and contained descriptors such as ninja, warrior, or superstar. They preferred words that described community and collaboration. Textio will run your job description through their software and will flag words they know will depress or attract the number of women or people of color who apply.

Humanyze, a company founded by Ben Waber, is based on the concepts of sociometrics, which creates tools that measure social relationships and embraces behavioral analytics. These can, among other things, look at the dynamics of meetings, predict attrition rates, and brainstorm ideas to ensure everyone is included.

Some of you may remember the 2011 movie *Moneyball,* based on Michael Lewis's best-selling book by the same name. It showed how baseball recruiters started using statistics and data in choosing the recruits for their teams. Scouts had always prided themselves on their stellar intuition when watching players for recruiting. For them, great baseball players had "the look," or they had heard great things about a young player, or they knew other scouts were interested. It turns out their intuition was partly valid, but was not the whole story, and the data augmented that intuition with formulas that could track patterns over time. Success at getting on-base turned out to be critical as a percentage of at-bat. Correlations that had never been made were easily made using data and turned out to be better predictors of a solid performer than decisions based solely on human, flawed, or incomplete information or perception.

Baseball, perhaps more than any other sport, thrives on using data. Companies could learn from the sport. As Daniel Kahneman wrote in his book *Thinking Fast and Slow*, "The hero of Lewis's book is Billy Beane, the manager of the Oakland A's, who made the unpopular decision to overrule the scouts and to select players by the statistics of past performance. The players the A's picked were inexpensive because other teams had rejected them for not looking the part. The team soon achieved excellent results at low cost."[9] It wasn't just low cost, it's that Beane was able to find the best and the true top players by using facts, not feelings.

Looking the part, whatever that part is, can lead us down a rabbit hole with consequences. Warren G. Harding, the 29th president of the United States, looked presidential, spoke like a president, and stood tall like a leader. He had a handsome appearance, was a nice guy, and dressed like a gentleman president should. He wanted to go back to the good old days and return to normalcy after World War I and the Spanish flu. Yet he was one of

---

[9] Daniel Kahneman, *Thinking, Fast and Slow* (Penguin, 2011).

the worst presidents the U.S. ever had—something he himself admitted.

We have archetypes of what people should look like, which we gather from our fairy tales and fables, from our textbooks, movies, songs, social media, our daily experiences, and the models presented to us. We have villains and heroes, and those we think of as weak and as strong. If someone fits into what our mind's eye believes is a positive role, they get to carry that benefit with them. If, however, our mind's eye conjures up negative images, the person who shares that image has an almost impossible task of overturning our prejudged thoughts. That's why we need help from both human and nonhuman guides as we work to remove those unconscious thoughts.

Kendall Wright, founder and CEO of Entelechy, talks about his work and a term he coined: cognitive suiting. "That is, how do we impose our expectations on others? Those expectations, of course, are driven by the unconscious bias. So, I dress you up the way that I think you ought to perform, the way that you ought to respond, where you ought to be in this hierarchy of opportunity. And as we look around our society, we are reminded that we judge people based on the uniform that they wear. And there's certain different expectations of a person who is dressed in a firefighter's uniform versus a person who is dressed in a first responder's uniform. So we have this cognitive, literally, projection of a suiting. I'm going to put this shirt on, I'm going to put this blouse on, I'm going to put this skirt on this person. And then you have this avatar of what do you think the person ought to do, where do they fit, and how they might contribute."

There are other externally imposed norms that act as tools to change behavior. These outside forces are essential overrides to the status quo and they come from laws, regulations, and changing what society permits or allows. So, one could argue that tools like quotas and affirmative mechanisms fall inside the rubric of nonhuman ways we overcome our own resistance to breaking the grip of our distorted beliefs. If, for example, voters think that women don't make as good leaders as men, then the hurdles for female candidates go above and beyond their positions on policy. It would be like two runners in a race, one wearing shoes that weigh a pound and another with shoes that weigh ten pounds. They both have the training, stamina, and skill, but the first runner has a 10-times greater advantage.

Support them or not, quotas and affirmative mechanisms force a balancing. It is an artificial and non-obstructable way to get change to occur. Asking people to change their unconscious beliefs may or may not work; we need outside ways, through data and people, to augment these beliefs, particularly when it comes to our ability to evaluate those who are not the same as us. There are emerging technologies that can help shape our behavior, such as the concept of working from home and what that technology allows us to do. The practice of working from home is not new, but it gained salience during the COVID-19 pandemic. Of course, many workers did not have the luxury of choosing to work from home during this hazardous time. You can't drive a bus remotely (not yet), sweep a factory floor, work at a chicken-packing plant, fight a fire, or provide hands-on treatment of a patient in the hospital from your computer at home.

But for many people, working from home was the only solution to keep organizations operating and people healthy. Technology kept up with the trend, making "to Zoom" a verb. Research is only just emerging about the impacts of working from home or a hybrid of in-person and at-home presence. Early indicators are that the ability to hire people who can work anywhere does mean that businesses will find it easier to create more diverse workplaces. Hiring can be from geographic places that have larger diverse demographics than a pool of workers from one city or town where the organization is located.

There is also growing awareness that virtual settings require additional management skills, such as making sure that everyone feels included on the calls and everyone is heard from (no different than the in-person meeting). Checking in with remote workers requires a studied equity, as does the doling out of work assignments, evenly distributed feedback, and hiring and performance review standards.

Technology can certainly be a boon and tool, as long as it comes with a cautionary user warning. For example, as mentioned, artificial intelligence techniques can enhance our decision-making but can also embed ongoing myths and beliefs about who people are.

When used wisely, technology can be another source of nonhuman but necessary assistance in our journey to create a more welcoming place for everyone. When it comes to fulfilling the value of diversity, equity, and inclusion, we are not alone in this effort. Like Dorothy, we can have support from those around us, and we can use the growing number of tools available to help us be our better selves.

Chapter 7

The Elephant and Mouse
Inclusive Leader

The Elephant and Mouse is fundamentally about how we look at the way organizations and people operate in diverse worlds. There are underlying assumptions built into this book.

The first assumption is that diversity is here to stay as a force and dynamic in our society. It may have fits and starts. It may get pushback from those who do not necessarily agree with how to embrace the changing world. But the world is changing. A company like Intel won't now use law firms with average or below average ratings on diversity. Ten years ago, that was an unthought of, if not unthinkable, criteria. And in the years to come, there will be even more that was unthinkable before as DEI morphs, evolves, and becomes more important. We will continue to learn more about individuals and how they experience the world. Social media continues to bring behaviors that were once unseen or hidden out into the open. Public opinion continues to move and reshape itself. DEI and social justice attitudes and demands can be considered a bellwether of those changes. DEI will force change and be forced by change.

The next essential step for the Elephant and Mouse leader is to move on to inclusion, to equity, to belongingness, to being valued, and to "ownership," as my colleagues Mason Donovan and Mark Kaplan of Dagoba Group frame it. This ownership notion is that we are all responsible for making our places of work (and ultimately society) diverse, equitable, and inclusive, with everyone feeling a sense of belonging. In their book, *The Inclusion Dividend*, the authors find a robust parallel with the requirement for a safe workplace to that of a diverse one.[1] Safety is often the highest priority in various industries such as the airlines, manufacturing, utilities, water companies, and construction, to name a few; every employee is responsible and "owns" that assurance of safety. Safety is measured constantly, at the most micro level, and training is continuous.

They tell the story of a CEO of a large industrial company whom an employee saw walking up a staircase, both hands loaded with files. The frontline employee advised the CEO that it meant breaking a safety protocol not to hold the handrail on the stairs. The CEO immediately thanked the employee for owning safety in that way and rearranged the papers in order to grab onto the stair rail.

For DEI, safety must also include the notion of what Amy Edmondson in 1999 called "psychological safety." This term references the idea that people will feel either

---

[1] Mason Donovan and Mark Kaplan, *The Inclusion Dividend : Why Investing in Diversity & Inclusion Pays Off* (Bibliomotion, 2013).

a high risk or a low risk for voicing their ideas, for making mistakes, or for bringing their full authentic selves to the workplace.[2] As humans, we want to avoid situations that have the potential to cause us to be negatively judged, to be excluded from the social group, to experience a loss of status, or to be penalized in some tangible way. This human reaction often translates into avoiding participation, sharing new ideas, admitting mistakes, or speaking up on difficult issues.

Elephants as a group will likely feel psychologically safe because the world they inhabit is one conceived by them. They know (and create) the rules, are often the judgers not the judged, and shape what is socially the norm. It is not usually necessary to hide parts of their self, to mask their differences to fit in (covering), to consciously reshape how they speak, or to take risks. They are assumed to belong. The Mouse may not have the same luxury of being assumed to belong, or to be able to make mistakes, or to be outside the norm.

For example, a 2017 study found that men were more likely to report that is was safe to take risks at work (38% strongly agreed or agreed) compared with women (29% strongly agreed or agreed).[3]

---

[2] Amy Edmondson, "Psychological Safety and Learning Behavior in Work Teams," *Administrative Science Quarterly* 44, no. 2 (1999): 350–83, https://www.jstor.org/stable/2666999.

[3] Australian Workplace Psychological Safety Survey, 2017.

The absence of psychological safety can be problematic to the point of danger. Employees may be less likely to speak up and challenge the behaviors of colleagues or their bosses or to challenge unsafe or dubious activities.

Elephant leaders must create environments that foster truth-telling and provide opportunities for all to produce new or different ideas without perception of negative reaction. Leaders may not realize the impact that they have on others. One incidence of dismissal of an idea or concern or embarrassing another can have a ripple effect throughout the workgroup.

Better would be for leaders to ask questions, reach out for other perspectives, ensure that someone is always playing a safe role as devil's advocate, seek out alternative explanations and solutions, and check the data. This is of particular importance in a diverse workplace. If one of the keystones of diversity is differing perspectives and experiences of the Mouse, then make sure the workplace encourages exactly those differences. The third assumption is that leadership will be with us in the near and future term. Hierarchies are not going away, though they may be taking on differing attributes shaped by the internal forces embedded in diverse organizations. There still will be those who are called upon to be at the forefront. They can be considered servant leaders, which has as its leitmotif the concept of leading from behind or having the purpose of enabling those they lead. Nevertheless, the word "leader" is not disappearing from any lexicon soon.

We may need to continue to ask what historian Samuel Huntington asked: leadership for what?

This book now takes up the leader who understands the Elephant and Mouse dynamic. Adam Grant is a brilliant organizational psychologist and best-selling author who focuses on how to create meaning at work and lead creative lives, lives that energize us, help us feel that we are significant and that what we do is important. In a 2021 World Economic Forum discussion, Grant was clear eyed in saying, "Leading in a diverse world is a competence, not a nice-to-have skill. We need to understand how to skill people to lead in inclusive ways and to understand that leading in a diverse world creates new demands."

Goldman Sachs (my former employer) has created an innovative curriculum for managers that equips new leaders with foundation and essential skills to foster inclusion on their teams. Kendall Wright posits that today's leaders need to humanize everyone they lead rather than view them as simple assets that produce what the company needs to create value for shareholders. Michael Useem, professor at the Wharton School of the University of Pennsylvania, calls this the need to create fresh capabilities for our current and future leaders.

Stephen Foster, CEO of Included, reflects that leaders need far more soft power than hard power, giving a nod to Joseph Nye, Jr., who set up the distinction that hard power represents a coercive approach to international relations and employs military or economic power to achieve certain outcomes.

Soft power, however, represents a subtle, persuasive approach to international relations between states. Leaders in any arena today need to embrace both hard and soft power, and in a diverse environment, soft power such as empathy and belonging become essential.

Many of us understand the need for emotional intelligence in leaders and the workplace. The term *emotional intelligence* was coined by two researchers, John Mayer and Peter Salovey.[4] As they described it, the term is "the subset of social intelligence that involves the ability to monitor one's own and others' feelings and emotions, to discriminate among them, and to use this information to guide one's thinking and actions." (It was later popularized by Dan Goleman in his book of the same name.[5])

We now need a further evolution of emotional intelligence skills, added to the lexicon of inclusive intelligence for traits we seek in leaders. I believe that the Elephant and Mouse construct can help guide us to ensuring the skills needed for the inclusive intelligence mandated by changing dynamics and forces in our world. The inclusive leader must demand new metrics for success, including

---

[4] John Mayer and Peter Salovey, "Emotional Intelligence," *Imagination, Cognition and Personality* 9, no. 3 (March 1, 1990), https://journals.sagepub.com/doi/10.2190/DUGG-P24E-52WK-6CDG.

[5] Daniel Goleman, *Emotional Intelligence: Why It Can Matter More Than IQ* (Bantam, 2006).

ensuring that all believe the organization is a meritocracy and feel a sense of belonging and ownership to accommodate the growing demand found in societies today for this more equitable and respectful world. The sea change for society must be reflected in a sea change for leaders and how they operate (and are rewarded) going forward.

"Before, we had leadership competencies that obviously relate within the inclusion space and what we believe is necessary for a leader to be effective in today's world," Mason Donovan said in my 2021 interview. "The one that we added in 2019 in the *Inclusion Dividend* became a standalone; it is creating a culture of ownership. And it's that culture of ownership that we find that is lacking, not just in inclusion, but often throughout the firm. How do you create that ownership culture in which people will interrupt that inappropriate behavior?"

For example, leaders are coming into a meeting and they're trying to break the ice by telling some stupid joke, and somebody at the table says, "Hey, you know, I don't think it's right to tell that joke." And then the leader says, "Ah, stop being such an x," (whatever word they want to use) and goes on to tell the joke. In that situation, the leader didn't receive the intervention well and has now created a whole new culture of how this is okay and critiquing a leader is not okay.

As a leader, you have to just be willing to own these issues and just act. Look at your team. Don't expect someone from HR to do this for you. Your HR or diversity folks should be your consultants, not your implementers. The organizations that tend to make the most progress have put the focus on individual leaders taking action within their span of influence.

Leadership theory and practice have evolved over time. Think about the transactional leader, the transformational leader, servant leader, and authentic leader. The evolution of leadership runs parallel to the evolution of societal norms, expectations, changing roles of organizations, and individual expectations. Many forces come into play. No longer useful are movie images like those seen in high action movies, like *The Fast and the Furious* (a series I admittedly do like) which show the good guy sustaining all sorts of attacks in a superhuman way while defeating the enemy after many car crashes. He may have a female sidekick or person of color with him, but he is the mastermind of the victory. Former U.S. President Donald Trump was known to say, "I alone can fix it." In fact, no leader alone can fix anything. It takes a village, as former U.S. Secretary of State Hillary Clinton often said. And we now know that it takes a diverse and inclusive village.

There are whole books and research papers that analyze how leadership and leaders have changed. The intent of this chapter is to reflect upon what must be added to any definition or requirement of leadership in organizations that embrace diversity, equity, inclusion, belonging, and justice. So, what now must be included as we think about who leaders need to be in this evolving and diverse world and how they must behave?

Self-awareness can top the list for all of us, but it is acutely needed for those who spearhead an inclusive environment. Understanding the concept of the Elephant and the Mouse is essential. That is, they must be aware that as leaders, and particularly those from dominant groups, they live in the world differently than others. They must recognize that the world doesn't operate for others as it operates for them. Having a clear-eyed understanding of other's lives becomes essential, particularly now that other diverse lives come from starkly different world experiences than in previous, more homogeneous times. Thus, the leader must be both actor and learner.

Leaders must also ensure DEI is included in all parts of the enterprise. Again, the Dagoba Group analogy of the safety priority can be illustrative. I worked for an airline long ago (TWA!), and managed both charter operations and airports in the western U.S. Safety was in everything we did, from the metrics to the minutest details. And *everyone* was responsible for ensuring that safety was the highest consideration. The ramp service person, the sales agent, the flight attendants, pilots, and mechanics were all crucial at every step of the way to achieve zero errors. Making note of problems, logging them, having the authority to stop a flight from taking off, fixing the defaults, calling out where someone was not following policy—this was the role of each of us, manager or nonmanager.

"Every leader has some latitude about what she decides what to do within the system," says Kendall Wright.

"And it's in that gray area of latitude that we then find these patterns of discrimination or exclusion or underutilization of a particular demographic. It's in the gray area of discretion, owned and occupied by the leader in the system."

Diversity has both micro and macro aspects to it. The macro includes the processes and systems embedded in the organization, such as recruitment strategies, promotion, or evaluation measures. It also entails micro behaviors (some call these micro aggressions or micro inclusions), which can be as simple as who gets invited to lunch with the boss and who doesn't. Basic sharing of information evenly within a group has an impact. Not allowing interruptions or providing more or less time for people to speak can be meaningful.

In previous chapters, I referenced how unlevel behavior in the workplace without leadership intervention, can lead to some ideas being over-heard and others being under-heard. Lydia Smith writes in Yahoo Finance UK:

> If you have ever found it difficult to get a word in edgeways in a meeting that mostly consists of men, you aren't alone.
>
> It's a situation that many women find themselves in at work. You have an idea that is relevant to the discussion, and you begin to speak—only to be interrupted or talked over by a male colleague. It's frustrating and common.

The old adage is that women talk more than men, but that doesn't hold true when it comes to work. There are scores of studies outlining the ways men dominate speaking in business-focused contexts, whether in morning meetings, conference calls, or academic seminars.

In 2017, Prattle studied more than 155,000 company conference calls over the past 19 years in research for Bloomberg, finding that men spoke 92% of the time. This is only partially explained by the dearth of women in executive roles—put frankly, it is also because men talk more.[6]

Elephant and Mouse leaders acquaint themselves with this type of research-based knowledge and act accordingly, making sure there is a more balanced speaking environment for dominant and nondominant group members. Leaders stay current with new research and understanding of the dynamics embedded in diverse workplace, much as they would anything related to their products and services.

Think about it: if you are a leader in any sector of business, philanthropy, or government, you would be

---

[6] Lydia Smith, "The Stark Reality of How Men Dominate Talking in Meetings," Yahoo!, April 10, 2019, https://www.yahoo.com/now/stark-reality-men-dominate-talking-meetings-113112910.html.

expected to keep up on the research and new discoveries in your work. Either you yourself would continue to stay informed or you would have others who digest updated knowledge on what is happening in your world to stay competitive or continue to meet client expectations. The E&M leader does that for the continually evolving world of diversity too. The best remain curious and questioning. When a statistic that shows men interrupt and talk over women more than women do to men, the E&M leader asks, "Is that happening in my organization?" If it is, they come up with solutions to remedy the problem, just as they would if being told that one of the products they are offering was manufactured with a defect.

Think about organizations that pledge to create sustainable practices. Every step in their value chain must reflect the concepts embraced by sustainability. New ideas and perspectives are key. Old ways can no longer be applied unthinkingly, and everyone must be 100% committed to these new practices.

So, DEI too requires the same commitment and integration into the everyday details of work life as safety and sustainability do. In this reading of safety and sustainability as the goals, it seems we then all become leaders. No one person can effectuate the change that is needed; no top of the hierarchy can have the answers that get transmitted to the implementers. The roles of active interventionist, wing person, and ally all take on greater significance.

The old model was that employers were used to being able to dictate when, where, and how employees work. The individual experiences of what was perceived as a homogeneous workforce were not made to count or even be noticed. This is no longer the case. Bryce Covert mentions that the perspective has changed. As one person he interviewed from Iceland said, "We are not just machines that just work. We are persons with desires and private lives, families and hobbies."[7] I would add we are also individuals with our own identities and our own lived experiences.

The Elephant and Mouse leader understands the pressures that are placed on those who are in the middle of the hierarchy. Ironically, these middle-layer individuals are caught between the Elephant above them and being the Mouse themselves. And yet they are also the Elephant to those who are below them in the hierarchy. As Jörg Schmitz, cultural anthropologist and business consultant at ThomasLeland, observed to me in 2021, those in the middle don't necessarily have the luxury of embracing DEI; they may feel themselves forced to do it or feel squeezed amidst the performance metrics they are measured on. They may even possess a discomfort in their mind between diversity goals and profit, performance, or other goals.

---

[7] Bryce Covert, "8 Hours a Day, 5 Days a Week Is Not Working for Us," *The New York Times*, July 20, 2021, https://www.nytimes.com/2021/07/20/opinion/covid-return-to-office.html.

The E&M leader recognizes these conflicting dynamics and balances the tools, metrics, and rewards to accommodate both the diversity and all of the other goals the organization has. The inclusive leader asks constantly, "What is missing and who is missing?" from their decision-making. You can't know what you don't know, or, as former U.S. Secretary of Defense Donald Rumsfeld would have called it, the "unknown unknowns." We reduce the probably of the unknown and therefore reduce the probability of making decisions on insufficient information, by bringing in those who, based on their lives and learnings, can help foreshadow and prevent unforced errors. These diverse perspectives can also be open to new possibilities, new products, services, and innovations.

Look today at any major supermarket company and you'll find products from other countries or cultures. In the U.S., there are now aisles full of food that have targeted appeal to the Hispanic, Latinx, and Asian communities as well as to vegans, vegetarians, pescatarian, and so on. If your world consisted of steak and potatoes growing up, you would have missed those expanding opportunities based on your own lived experiences.

The more recognition of and voice for the diversity of the world, the less any one of us can see the full picture, limited as we are by our own telescopes. My own homogeneous group cannot operate and dominate in this world because, among other things, talent, customers, ideas, and markets are no longer homogeneous. Actually, they never were; it is the realization that has changed.

However, what does remain homogeneous and becomes the work of the E&M leader to ensure is the homogeneity of commitment, values, mission, reality of meritocracy, inclusion, and equity.

I would be remiss in this chapter on the new leader if I did not discuss the issue of women's and men's leadership. This is a topic I have spent much of my career focused upon, whether it was from interacting with women heads of state and government, observing and hearing from many women leaders, or writing and lecturing on it. Much has been written on the topic and on leadership models such as the ATHENA Leadership Model (ATHENA International) or that of the Vital Voices Leadership Model. These models often stress traits that are seen as ones that women are more likely to bring to bear, such as compassion, empathy, authenticity, and inclusion. The ATHENA model for women embraces the learning leader, the advocate who acts courageously, builds relationships, and fosters collaboration.

KPMG further notes that women leaders seem more adaptable to change than men, more likely to use situational leadership behaviors based on the situation and facts on hand, or to ask for feedback and listen. They may be more likely to read a room and note unspoken nonverbal cues.[8]

---

[8] KPMG Women's Leadership Summit, "Women Executives Believe They Must Adjust Their Leadership Style More Often Than Men to Advance," KPMG, June 19, 2019, https://womensleadership.kpmg.us/kpmg-womens-leadership-report.html/?utm_source=USATODAY &utm_content=Article4.

This latter trait, as referenced before, often called "female intuition," is the classic nondominant Mouse learned behavior. It is hypervigilance of the nondominant group, always being highly watchful of the other, given the necessity of it to stay out of harm's way and the value of it to advance its own goals. For many women, tragically, that hypervigilance becomes a survival technique when they are faced with abuse or violence.

At times, when these traits are articulated, people respond to me with the "what about" scenario, as in what about Margaret Thatcher. She seemed on the face of it to have little compassion, collaboration, or listening skills. Her moniker was "Iron Lady." She definitely took on the characteristics of the species she wanted to invade.

This "what about" question is invariably the issue of possibility and frequency. One can always come up with the opposite example of what is being posited. This is the common note that the exception proves the rule. Yes, plenty of women may take on more male attributes, but the group as a whole will behave in the ways that they have learned, have been given social approval for, and have found useful in living and leading.

Generally speaking, women are less risk tolerant than men, with most research focused on financial risk taking.[9] Women and people of color have experienced

---

[9] "Life Differences Make Women Less Risk Tolerant When Investing," ScienceDaily, September 20, 2017, https://www.sciencedaily.com/releases/2017/09/170920131727.htm.

the penalty of taking risks and are less likely to want to expose themselves or their assets to potentially higher levels of loss. The COVID-19 pandemic required choices about what risks countries were going to take. Women leaders of countries potentially saw the need to react with more conservative measures more quickly, such as lockdowns and quarantines, and listened to the science as it developed.

Bottom line: I do believe that women bring some practices to leadership that should be embraced by men. Similarly, there are leadership practices that men use that would be of help to women. The Elephant, for example, goes where it wants to, is not afraid to speak its mind, isn't so worried about what others think or perceive about them, and has the size and power to withstand more risky behavior. The Mouse is more aware of what the other is experiencing, is more vigilant to the dynamics of the situation, and won't risk as easily as the stakes are higher.

My fundamental belief is that the best leaders have the most tools in their toolbox to respond to changing situations. For example, there are times when command-and-control transaction leadership is needed, such as when the building is burning. There are other occasions, however, when consensus collaboration is the best approach when coming up with innovation and creativity. The great leaders know when to choose what.

One cautionary note in the challenge for women embracing some of men's styles is that they may not get a warm reception to those actions and instead may receive negative social consequences for their behavior, whereas men get to have the full panoply of behaviors of both Elephant and Mouse with little likelihood of penalty.

Finally, in thinking about what is required now for the leader of the diverse and inclusive future, who understands and practices both Elephant and Mouse awareness, understanding, metrics, equitable processes, and inclusive behaviors, consider this simple chart:

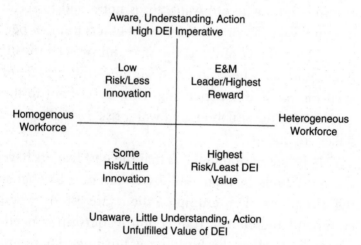

This chart expresses my belief that the best leaders—both men and women—have a keen understanding of what their diverse workforce experiences, and measures gaps between the differing groups of their work experiences. They acutely grasp the dynamics of Elephant and Mouse. The upper right quadrant leader gets the most out of the diverse teams, communicating and holding accountable the imperative of a truly inclusive workplace with the urgency they would express if it were a safety issue, or the need to provide a service that works best with zero defects or errors (any organization in fact).

In the beginning of this book, I reflected on the hard truths of the journey of diversity, equity, and inclusion. In the scope of history and society, these goals are relatively new to humanity. Yet today so much attention is focused on wanting to create a fairer world, more sustainable and just. No doubt these goals will be a continuous journey with rapid or slow progress at different times, perhaps even setbacks. For me, the concepts included in the Elephant and Mouse are part of the tapestry of progress. Ten years from now there will be even more knowledge of what is needed. My hope for those who are committed to DEI and want to hurry history is that this book has helped them on their journey.

Bibliography

Ammerman, Colleen, and Boris Groysberg. *Glass Half Broken*. Harvard Business Review Press, 2021.

Bohnet, Iris. *What Works: Gender Equality By Design*. Belknap Harvard, 2016.

Chamorro-Premuzic, Tomas. *Why So Many Incompetent Men Become Leaders*. Harvard Business Review Press, 2019.

Dhir, Aaron. *Challenging Boardroom Homogeneity*. Cambridge Press, 2015.

Doyle-Morris, Suzanne. *The Con Job*. Wit & Wisdom Press, 2020.

Grant, Adam. *Originals*. Penguin, 2014.

Halpern, David. *Inside the Nudge Unit: How Small Changes Can Make a Big Difference*. WH Allen, 2015.

Kahneman, Daniel. *Thinking Fast and Slow*. FSG, 2011.

Kay, Kathy, and Claire Shipman. *The Confidence Code*. Harper Business, 2014.

Kendi, Ibram X. *How to Be an Anti-Racist*. One World, 2019.

Sandburg, Sheryl. *Lean In*. Alfred A. Knopf, 2013.

Wilkerson, Isabel. *Caste*. Random House, 2020.

About the Author

Laura Liswood is the secretary general of the Council of Women World Leaders, which is composed of women presidents and prime ministers, and is the former managing director and senior advisor for Global Leadership and Diversity at Goldman Sachs. After the events of 9/11, she became a reserve police officer for the Washington, DC, Metropolitan Police Department for thirteen years and retired as a sergeant. She is also the author of *The Loudest Duck: Moving Beyond Diversity to Achieve Success in the Workplace*.

Index

174

Index